McKinsey Quarterly

2011 Number 1

This Quarter

For many of us, the start of a new year is a time
for resolutions. Some are purely personal, while others
reflect the opportunities and challenges facing our
organizations. In this first *McKinsey Quarterly* of 2011,
we offer insights on three priorities that reflect the
diversity of issues our clients are dealing with in these
still uncertain times: pressure testing your company's
strategy, boosting the flexibility of your supply chain,
and enhancing personal productivity. While un-
doubtedly not the only issues you'll be grappling with,
they're timely, important, and universal enough that
we've devoted all of this issue's features section to them.

This year, many companies will likely pursue new sources of growth.
Doing so profitably, even in higher-growth emerging markets,
often requires a new formula for competitive advantage and a new
deployment of resources—a revisiting of a company's strategy,
in short. To help in that effort, my colleagues Chris Bradley, Martin
Hirt, and Sven Smit introduce ten tests that any leader can use
to stir up strategic dialogue in his or her organization. In addition,

four senior executives share the tough questions they like to ask. Kicking the tires on your strategic direction can help avoid what UCLA management professor Richard Rumelt calls "bad strategy" in the excerpt we present here from his forthcoming book, *Good Strategy/ Bad Strategy: The Difference and Why It Matters.*

The combination of globalization and economic uncertainty in many product markets presents a particular challenge to companies that buy and sell physical goods. They need a supply chain that will be economic under a variety of circumstances—a revaluation of the renminbi, a new carbon tax, and dramatic shifts in the importance of different markets, to name a few. Actually, say Yogesh Malik, Alex Niemeyer, and Brian Ruwadi, of McKinsey's operations practice, companies need several supply chains, each configured to cope with rising levels of complexity and to hedge against uncertainty. Pulling this off requires serious collaboration across the C-suite, a topic addressed in the related article, "Is your top team undermining your supply chain?"

Finally, if we can all count on one thing this year, it is the unending demands on our time from an onslaught of information that's both valuable and distracting. In an article that seems heretical for two busy leaders, McKinsey alumnus Derek Dean and Caroline Webb, of McKinsey's organization practice, explain why coping through multitasking doesn't work and propose alternatives for over-burdened executives. Of course, senior managers aren't the only ones who need new ways of working. In "Rethinking knowledge work: A strategic approach," Tom Davenport of Babson College offers a road map for helping knowledge workers across the organization cope with information overload.

Even if these challenges don't make your top-three list for the new year, we hope that pondering them helps you stay focused on the sort of big, long-term priorities that often get overshadowed by day-to-day operating concerns. Certainly, we promise to keep exploring issues like these in our continuing effort to help inform the global senior-management agenda. o

David Court
Director, Dallas Office

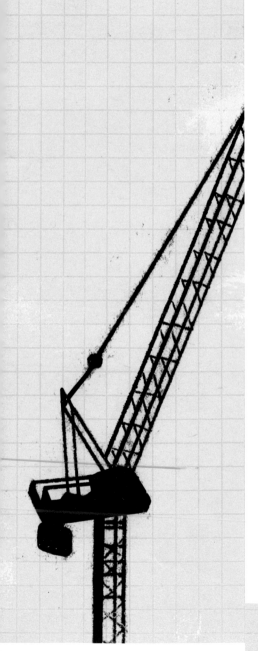

On the cover
Constructing your 2011 agenda

Boost supply chain resiliency

Stop the madness of knowledge work

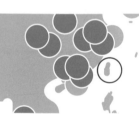
Departments

Leading Edge

Applied Insight

McKinsey On the Web

Now available on
mckinseyquarterly.com

Creating value:
An interactive tutorial

In this video presentation, McKinsey partner Tim Koller explores the four guiding principles of corporate finance that all executives can use to home in on value creation when they make strategic decisions.

Video and audio podcasts on iTunes
Download conversations with executives and authors in audio or video from iTunes.
audio: http://bit.ly/mckinseyitunesaudio
video: http://bit.ly/mckinseyitunesvideo

**Join the *McKinsey Quarterly*
community on Facebook**
facebook.com/mckinseyquarterly

Follow us on Twitter
Receive notification of new content by following @McKQuarterly on Twitter.

Download this issue
for free from Zinio

Read this issue of *McKinsey Quarterly* on your iPad, iPhone, or computer (PC or Mac). http://bit.ly/mckinseydigitalissue

For iPhones, you may also use your QR scanning application to access this issue.

Other features:

Do you have a long-term
pricing strategy?

Actively pricing products across their life cycle is increasingly important, particularly in innovation-intensive industries. Failing to do so may forego potential profits or even destroy value.

Moving women to the top:
McKinsey Global Survey results

A majority of executives believe gender diversity in leadership is linked to better financial performance, but companies take few actions to support women in the workforce.

The rise of the networked
enterprise: Web 2.0 finds its payday

McKinsey's new survey research finds that companies using the Web intensively gain greater market share and higher margins.

Idea Exchange

Readers mix it up with authors of articles from *McKinsey Quarterly*
2010, Number 4

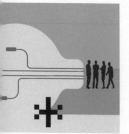

Clouds, big data, and smart assets:

Ten tech-enabled business trends to watch

The cover story in our previous issue focused on the management
implications of technology trends now under way. The following is a brief
exchange between a reader and one of the authors of the article.

Jaime Batiz

Tech director, AOL Advertising, Mountain View, California

"As someone working in the front lines of research, implementation, and operation of data-driven technology for the Internet advertising industry, I see that
most of these emerging trends have been the status quo for several quarters.
It is interesting to see other fields where they will create strongholds. A common
denominator in all of them is that companies that don't work in these ways
now will face great inertial forces to change. Surely some will succeed, but I
believe these trends are more likely to guide entrepreneurs looking for the
next great success story."

McKinsey's Jacques Bughin responds:

"Taken together, the various trends of our article will indeed induce companies—
small or large, global or local—to operate under a new paradigm. It is somewhat of a myth, however, that only small attackers and entrepreneurs will be
successful in doing this. According to the Marketing Science Institute, schol-
ars who systematically looked at the introduction of disruptive technologies in
a large set of markets worldwide concluded that rather than small entrants
or entrepreneurs, it's more often incumbents that disrupt their own markets by
innovating in new business models for growth.

In our work to understand the trends more deeply, we also have been surprised
by the number of large companies starting to excel at benefitting from them.
A hallmark case is P&G, one of the first to institutionalize a word-of-mouth influence model, with Tremor. It also launched its Connect + Develop platform to
cocreate new products with users. In general, inertial forces to change exist—
the imperative to act against the treadmill is thus critical—but large companies actually have more skills and assets to leverage for the new trends than they
realize. The trick here is to discover those capabilities and decide to change."

Visit **mckinseyquarterly.com** to share your
own comments or see more from our readers on these
and other topics.

How centered leaders achieve extraordinary results

In the previous issue of *McKinsey Quarterly*, we published two articles and a survey that explored the relationship between personal values and leadership traits. This material generated significant discussion on mckinseyquarterly.com. A small portion appears here in edited form.

Energizing 'Generation Y' workers

Svetlana Zhukova
Digital marketing manager, Australia Council for the Arts, Sydney

"I completely agree with 'meaning' having a very strong impact not just for business but for personal happiness as well. Increasingly, it is important for all employees, and in particular for Gen Y, to believe that what they do has value. Best achievements happen when leaders believe in what they and their companies do—enthusiasm is contagious—and, often, meaning motivates as well as (or better than) financial rewards."

McKinsey's Joanna Barsh responds:

"Our recent survey research revealed an interesting finding: both women and men in their 30s have dramatically lower 'energizing' scores than do members of other age groups. It goes without saying, but individuals who experience low energy at work will ultimately choose to go—and companies that churn out their young people will eventually find themselves without a workforce or with a workforce that is challenging to manage. In teaching centered leadership at workshops around the world, we find Gen Yers eager to make a difference and inspired by this leadership journey. It is not too late for those in charge to inspire their employees and unlock greater potential."

Sources of meaning

Aravind Vasudevan
Supply chain manager, Novelis AG, Zurich

"Going through the research results, it is revealing to see that 'meaning' plays such a significant role in leadership. As corporate leaders, what is the essence of meaning? Why should a corporate leader believe that the dynamics of selling soft drinks has a higher purpose in order to be a great leader? It is not clear how such intangible assets could be translated into real meaning for corporate leaders."

McKinsey's Josephine Mogelof and Caroline Webb respond:

"Meaning is very personal, and we make no judgment about its source. Even if one struggles to find meaning in a job, there is plenty of meaning in building a business that provides jobs for people, that supports the professional and personal development of its employees, that inspires individuals to innovate, and that gives back to its community. Regardless of where your meaning comes from, we would underscore one suggestion: don't make the mistake of assuming the people on your team obtain meaning from similar sources. Help them on their journeys and then work together to find common aspirations you can collectively work toward. When you do that, the team's potential will have increased by an order of magnitude."

Leading Edge

The fast lane to the adoption of electric cars

Russell Hensley, Stefan M. Knupfer, and Axel Krieger

Large cities may be the ideal test track for the mass market. Catalyzing early adoption
could take less than most auto executives and policy makers think.

As more and more electrified vehicles hit the floors of car dealerships, conventional wisdom has it that the market won't get moving without richer incentives and dense battery-charging networks.

Yet our research on demand for electric cars in very large urban areas[1] shows that plug-in hybrid electric vehicles and battery-only electric vehicles could account for 16 percent of overall new-car sales in New York, 9 percent in Paris, and 5 percent in Shanghai by 2015. That's true even with today's financial incentives and limited public charging facilities.[2]

It's not surprising that the market may take root in big cities: nowhere is the need for cleaner air and reduced carbon dioxide emissions more pressing, and nowhere else can you expect to find as many green-minded early adopters who will welcome a clean vehicle that takes them the short distances they need to go on one charge. These characteristics make large urban areas the ideal labs for the next phase of electric-vehicle development. Our research offers insights that can guide auto companies, battery makers, infrastructure providers, and city governments alike as they consider moving forward with this technology and the networks that support it.

Large markets are waiting to be served. We found big clusters of potential early adopters— 30 percent of all car buyers in Shanghai and 20 percent in New York—who were distinguished by their green thinking and would consider buying an electric car.

For early adopters, the charging problem isn't as big as it seems. Unlike other groups of car buyers in New York and Shanghai, early adopters were willing to adjust their driving and parking habits to own an electric car. In fact, they indicated that a dense public charging infrastructure would only modestly increase their interest in buying

Drivers in New York, Paris, and Shanghai generally prefer plug-in hybrids.

Electric-vehicle type

■ Plug-in hybrid (PHEV)   ■ Battery only (BEV)   ■ Electric city car (a subset of BEV)[1]

Projected 2015 demand for electric vehicles by city

	% of new car sales	Number of electric vehicles
New York	9 1 6 16	~70,000
Paris	7 2 9	~62,000
Shanghai	5 <1 ~5	~26,000

[1] Tested in New York and Shanghai but not in Paris.

such cars and that they were willing to cope with more limited charging options. This attitude reduces the need for public investments in the start-up stage, though a broad plug-in infrastructure will no doubt be critical as electrified vehicles migrate to mass adoption in large cities and elsewhere.

This is also good news for automakers, which have the opportunity to overcome another major obstacle: battery limits. Since many drivers in large cities travel only short distances—to and from work, for instance—the near-term cost and duration of electric-car batteries is less of a problem there than it is elsewhere. Rather than offering only all-purpose electric vehicles, automakers can segment buyers according to their driving missions and develop attractively priced models with no more battery energy storage than many of their city drivers need.

Technology preferences vary between cities. Shanghai buyers overwhelmingly preferred plug-in hybrid electric vehicles, which can drive some 60 kilometers (about 40 miles) on one charge and then switch to a gasoline-powered engine. The reason is the large share of first-time car buyers in Shanghai who demand family-size cars with full functionality. In New York, though, small electric city cars—a type of battery-only vehicle that can go 60 to 90 kilometers on a full charge—turned out to be very popular.

Design matters, but in different ways. Most buyers in New York and Shanghai look for status: being the first with the latest technology and standing out from the crowd. But residents of Shanghai would like a novel and distinctive design, while New Yorkers prefer a more conventional design, albeit with the attributes that identify a vehicle as an electric car.

Nonfinancial incentives can be surprisingly effective. The smartest way to get the market going isn't necessarily by increasing financial incentives. We found that monetary incentives, such as the US federal tax credit of up to $7,500 on the purchase of an electric car, will help stimulate initial demand. Yet raising them considerably will not lead to a quantum leap in adoption. In fact, among the 30 financial and non-financial measures we tested with New York consumers, some low-cost options were surprisingly effective.

Consumer education is one such measure that will be critical for catalyzing both early and mass adoption. Forty percent of

Few respondents in New York and Shanghai knew that battery-powered cars can potentially accelerate faster than conventional ones.

Some low-cost policy levers can significantly boost electric-vehicle adoption.

Levers directly relevant for New York City

▶ **Height of column indicates cost per additional electric vehicle (EV) adopted**
in excess of those that would be adopted with no levers pulled, $ thousand

▶ **Width of column indicates relative impact**
(wider = greater impact)[1]

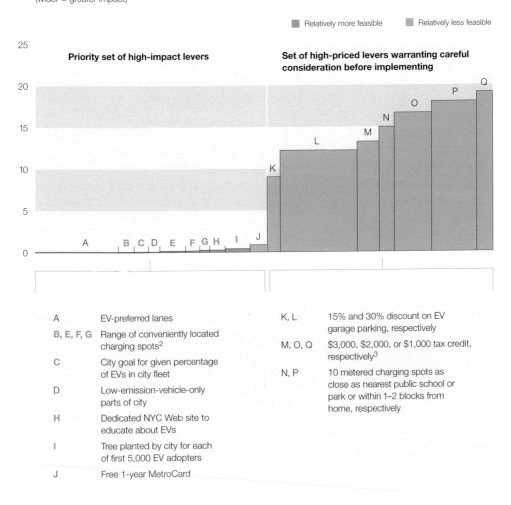

A	EV-preferred lanes
B, E, F, G	Range of conveniently located charging spots[2]
C	City goal for given percentage of EVs in city fleet
D	Low-emission-vehicle-only parts of city
H	Dedicated NYC Web site to educate about EVs
I	Tree planted by city for each of first 5,000 EV adopters
J	Free 1-year MetroCard

K, L	15% and 30% discount on EV garage parking, respectively
M, O, Q	$3,000, $2,000, or $1,000 tax credit, respectively[3]
N, P	10 metered charging spots as close as nearest public school or park or within 1–2 blocks from home, respectively

[1] Impact defined as 1 additional EV adopted as a result of lever being pulled; incremental impacts of levers are not additive.
[2] B = charging spots available in commercial garages, E = in central locations, F = in commuter stations and major junctions, G = 10 metered charging spots within 2 miles of home.
[3] At lower levels, tax credits are extended to more people who would have adopted EVs anyway, creating a higher cost per additional incremental adoption.

New York and Shanghai respondents said they didn't know much about electric vehicles and many were anxious about driving-range limitations. Few knew that battery-powered cars are relatively quiet and can potentially accelerate faster than conventional ones. And more important, many weren't aware that electric cars help drivers save money on both fuel and maintenance in the long run.

•   •   •

So what comes next? Highly motivated private users in large cities such as New York and Shanghai—along with other potential early adopters, such as drivers of inner-city delivery vans with fixed routes—will be key to the electric-vehicle market's longer-term development. By tailoring early products to the needs of these segments, automakers can build a strong base of core buyers whose use will spread word of mouth and drive market momentum. This approach, if supported with targeted actions by national and city governments, power providers, and battery makers, could accelerate the mass production and broad adoption of electric vehicles. ○

[1] The study of potential private users of electric cars, conducted in late 2009, was a joint effort by McKinsey, the city authorities of New York and Shanghai, and the French government. Efforts in New York and Shanghai focused on consumer research, including qualitative research that involved individual and group interviews, as well as an extensive quantitative survey of more than 1,000 potential buyers in New York and more than 600 in Shanghai. The Paris research team developed a comprehensive market model to project demand for the greater metropolitan region.

[2] The projections take into account expert forecasts of key drivers, such as the price of oil and the cost of electric-car batteries, a limited number of electric-vehicle brands and models available for sale during the time period, a set of incentives (for example, in New York a federal tax credit of up to $7,500 on purchases of electric cars), and a lack of existing public infrastructure for charging car batteries.

Russell Hensley is a principal in McKinsey's Detroit office; **Stefan Knupfer** is a director in the Stamford office, where **Axel Krieger** is a principal.

For more on defining the future market for electric cars, see "A new segmentation for electric vehicles," on mckinseyquarterly.com.

The Web's €100 billion surplus

Jacques Bughin

Consumers get the bulk of it with free services like social networks. Will industry dynamics shift as providers and advertisers try to get a bigger share?

Consumers derive significant value from all they do on the Web, and since advertising pays for much of this, it involves no immediate out-of-pocket cost. We all experience these benefits each time we log onto a social network or watch a free Web video.

But how much is all of this Web use worth? About €150 billion a year, according to new McKinsey research involving a survey of 4,500 Web users across Europe and the United States, as well as conjoint analysis of their willingness to pay for various online activities.[1]

Consumers *do* pay for some of this: €30 billion for services such as music subscriptions and gaming Web sites. In a sense, they also pay for the "pollution" of their Internet experience by intrusive pop-up advertising and perceived data privacy risks, an amount we estimate to be €20 billion after asking consumers what they would pay to avoid further clutter and privacy concerns. That leaves a substantial consumer surplus of €100 billion a year, a total that we project will grow to €190 billion by 2015 as broadband becomes ubiquitous around the world and as new services and wireless devices come to the fore.

For Web service providers, this is a large parcel of value to leave on the table. In fact, it amounts to more than three times the €30 billion companies pay providers to advertise on their Web sites and is almost as much as the €120 billion consumers pay for wired and wireless broadband access. One reason for this seeming largesse may be that once a Web service is created, the cost of distributing it is very low, and most Web companies are satisfied covering their basic costs with advertising. In the offline world, things are different, of course: the surplus is more evenly divided between consumers and suppliers, since in many markets—books, movies, or cable TV, for example—consumers pay for content.

Three ways Web economics could shift

Web players may try to recapture some of this large, growing source of value. One not-too-distant example of such a move is how

Four Internet services generate 52 percent of the consumer surplus created on the Web.

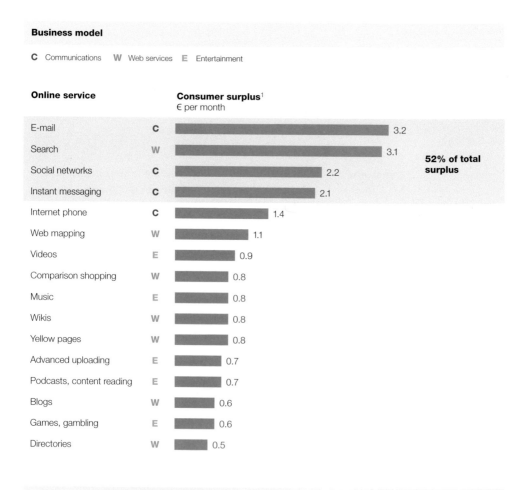

Business model

C Communications   **W** Web services   **E** Entertainment

Online service		Consumer surplus[1] € per month
E-mail	C	3.2
Search	W	3.1
Social networks	C	2.2
Instant messaging	C	2.1
Internet phone	C	1.4
Web mapping	W	1.1
Videos	E	0.9
Comparison shopping	W	0.8
Music	E	0.8
Wikis	W	0.8
Yellow pages	W	0.8
Advanced uploading	E	0.7
Podcasts, content reading	E	0.7
Blogs	W	0.6
Games, gambling	E	0.6
Directories	W	0.5

52% of total surplus

Surplus share by business model

Communications 44%
Web services 38%
Entertainment 18%

[1] Surplus is derived from estimated value of consumer service minus the price for paid services and the amount a consumer is willing to pay, both to avoid being disturbed by advertising formats and to limit private-information abuse while using ad-funded Internet services.

Source: IAB Europe; McKinsey analysis

As more business and individual activities move online, early movers should be well positioned to capture higher ad revenues and perhaps, over time, higher service fees.

Advertising grows

Another strategy would be to ramp up Web advertising, and here, the "pollution factor" may be the key. At present, Web companies are reaping more in advertising revenues than consumers are willing to pay to avoid them (€30 billion versus €20 billion). This imbalance suggests that today's levels of advertising are sustainable and that there could be room for more ads or other monetization plays, such as asking consumers to provide more personal data to access services.

It's hard to say how much more, though, because there's no data on how consumers would respond if Web pollution grew a great deal. Is there a tipping point where their willingness to pay to eliminate pollution would increase so dramatically that business models would shift in response? For example, if ad revenue grew to €40 billion or €50 billion, it is not clear whether consumers' willingness to pay to avoid the new ads would grow so much that Web service providers would be better able to extract more surplus by charging users more, as opposed to selling still more ads.

broadcasters gradually shifted service from free programming to pay-TV to capture a bigger slice of value. While it's not clear how things will play out on the Web, at least three scenarios seem worth contemplating.

Service costs rise

One obvious possibility is that Web players will charge more for services, they already do for certain premium offerings, such as multiplayer video game sites or subscription-based access to unlimited music libraries. So far there's been strong resistance to this approach from consumers: only about 20 percent of online users pay for some services, and our research shows that expanding the scope of fees to an amount equaling the value of the surplus would reduce usage by as much as 50 percent, torpedoing the economics of Web services.

Monetization by other means

Web players operate in multisided markets that allow them to collect revenues from both their advertisers and their users. They may be betting that by creating a large consumer surplus today with free services and big audiences, they will bolster their online brands, leading to higher profits or market value down the road. The rationale for this approach is pretty compelling, though a for-pay walled garden would work only for premium brands and services. Even for those, reach will be limited—as will companies' ability to use their Web platforms to launch other businesses.

Preparing for change

Of course, we're still in the early days of the Web economy, and only recently has the consumer surplus swelled with the rise of blockbusters such as Facebook and always-on connectivity. Clearly, this is a market that's far from equilibrium, so players should be planning for major change and preparing their strategies accordingly.

Service players trying to stay ahead of market shifts must be attuned to rapid market consolidation: the top 100 providers accounted for 45 percent of Web traffic in 2010, up from only 20 percent in 2007. To stay ahead, leading players are already broadening their base of services on robust proprietary platforms, particularly services that can be offered at low cost via the cloud and mobile devices; Twitter and Facebook are prime examples of such multiuse platforms. As more business and individual activities move online, early movers should be well positioned to capture higher advertising revenues and perhaps, over time, higher service fees.

In turn, advertisers may have better revenue options because of Web innovations. Some are already moving beyond distracting display ads; they're designing branded content promotions to attract the attention of users and shaping marketing campaigns around messages that travel virally among socially networked "friends," thus making these campaigns more acceptable to the consumer.

For consumers, the benefits of Web surpluses will continue. Engagement with consumers is the key to value creation in multisided markets, so they should expect continuing service innovations and tolerable advertising levels that keep the prices for Web use and access low. ○

[1] Because users pay a flat rate to access free services, we used a conjoint-analysis technique to help unbundle the willingness to pay for services from access. The value of services in the conjoint analysis was compared with the cost of advertising interruption as well as the value of online privacy.

Jacques Bughin is a director in McKinsey's Brussels office.

The commodity crunch in consumer packaged goods

Richard Benson-Armer, Peter Czerepak, and Tim Koller

Packaged-goods companies have been socked by rising commodity prices. Executives in other industries can learn from their experience.

For almost 40 years, the US consumer goods sector was among the safest of havens for investors. It rewarded them with annual returns well above the market average—second only to those of the energy sector—and in a bumper period from 1985 to 2002 outperformed the S&P 500 index by almost 20 percent annually. Since then, the sector has barely outpaced the index, despite persistent attempts by companies to find winning strategies. While inadequate cost controls and a failure to deliver significant value from a wave of mergers and acquisitions haven't helped, one factor is the dominant culprit for the current malaise: the industry's response to changing commodity prices.

Losing control

From 1985 to 2002, consumer-packaged-goods companies regularly passed on to consumers increases in the price of inputs (including aluminum, cereals, oil, and paper) while holding the line on prices when raw-material costs declined. In this way, these companies main-tained profit margins when input costs rose and enjoyed expanding margins when they fell. In fact, we estimate that between 1996 and 2002, the strategy of passing on commodity price increases was responsible for two-thirds of net margin expansion in the sector, or roughly $10 billion in value.

The tables turned in 2002. From that year until 2007, industry players passed on price increases of just 15 percent as cumulative commodity costs grew by 40 percent. As a result, we estimate that the failure to pass on commodity price increases was responsible, during that period, for 75 percent of the sector's margin contraction, which cost about $70 billion.[1]

A return to the days of passing commodity price increases on to consumers won't come easily. The structural shifts that dampened the industry's pricing power remain: consumers are increasingly value conscious, and large discounters still dominate the retail landscape. These retailers, using detailed analysis of data available from their point-of-sales systems and shopper research, today have a sophisticated understanding of the prices they want and of their ability to demand those prices.

The net result is that the industry continues to face downward pressure on prices. Some of the solutions aren't complicated, but they are extremely difficult to implement and probably hold lessons for companies—in sectors ranging from consumer electronics to industrial chemicals to medical devices— currently facing an unfavorable and volatile environment for raw-material costs and pricing.

Regaining the initiative

Many economists and financial-market forecasters believe that continued price volatility amid a general rise in commodity prices is likely as the world economy recovers, so companies across many sectors may easily destroy value in the years ahead. Suppose that in consumer packaged goods, commodity prices

Since 2002, industry players in packaged goods have been less able to pass input price increases on to consumers.

Consumer-packaged-goods industry,
index: product price index and raw-material price in 1985 = 100

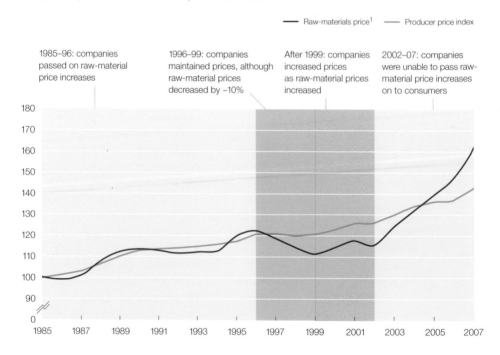

——— Raw-materials price[1]   ——— Producer price index

1985–96: companies passed on raw-material price increases

1996–99: companies maintained prices, although raw-material prices decreased by ~10%

After 1999: companies increased prices as raw-material prices increased

2002–07: companies were unable to pass raw-material price increases on to consumers

[1] Average weighted by sector-specific indexes for raw-material inputs—eg, aluminum, plastics, and raw sugarcane as inputs for soft drinks—and by weight of sector in overall consumer-packaged-goods market.

Source: Standard & Poor's Compustat; US Bureau of Labor Statistics; McKinsey analysis

increase by about 20 percent during the next five years, and companies hold prices constant in a quest to maintain market share. In that case, up to 4.5 percentage points of margin could be lost—or about 33 percent of current earnings before interest, taxes, depreciation, and amortization (EBITDA). Avoiding this fate will require iron-willed pricing resolve, which may be richly rewarded if the environment turns slightly more favorable. If commodity prices fall by 5 percent in the next five years but companies hold product prices steady, for example, we estimate that industry margins will increase by around 1 percentage point, and EBITDA will jump by 8 percent, reversing the current trend.

Conceiving, developing, and marketing category-changing products that consumers crave has long been the lifeblood of leading consumer-packaged-goods companies—and, for that matter, a priority for companies in a great many industries. An important question for all is how to capitalize on the opportunity that such innovations present to reset prices upward across relevant product categories, as P&G managed to do when the company introduced its Swiffer cleaning product. Capitalizing on innovations isn't easy. But in an industry like packaged goods,

it's probably critical for companies that aim for a financially sustainable innovation pipeline, for consumers who seek a steady stream of new products that satisfy new needs, and for retailers that hope to benefit from greater demand for new and existing products. ○

[1] Our analysis excludes 2008 and 2009, when the global recession and dramatic market fluctuations skewed the data.

Richard Benson-Armer is a director in McKinsey's New Jersey office, **Peter Czerepak** is an associate principal in the Boston office, and **Tim Koller** is a principal in the New York office.

For related thinking on pricing products across their life cycle, see "Do you have a long-term pricing strategy?" on mckinseyquarterly.com.

China's new pragmatic consumers

Yuval Atsmon and Max Magni

As incomes rise, China's consumers combine a taste for better products with a strong element of frugality.

Increasingly, China's urban consumers are looking more like affluent buyers in other corners of the globe. As the nation's wealth grows, shoppers are trading up to higher-quality branded goods. In fact, fully half of total consumption growth in China over the past year resulted from "trade up" purchases (where consumers bought the same amount of a particular product but at a higher quality and price), according to McKinsey research involving surveys of 15,000 Chinese consumers in 49 cities.[1]

Trading up is common in both developed and emerging markets and is often enabled by a rise in buying on credit. Consumers in China, on the other hand, typically finance trading up with what we call "trading off," which involves reducing spending in other categories. Our research suggests that fully 50 percent of Chinese households balance their trade-up purchases with spending reductions elsewhere.

Consumers who traded up in one to three categories traded down in as many as seven others. Some 80 percent of trade-up demand

for higher-quality clothing, shoes, and accessories came not from China's high-income "fashionistas" but rather from lower-middle-income consumers looking either to impress job interviewers or advertise their ascent from the working to the consumer class. Similarly, more than 70 percent of trade-up spending for dining out and 50 percent for alcohol come from white-collar men who want to improve their standing with clients or colleagues. To balance their overall spending, they trade down on personal-care products and packaged snack foods. This distinctive blend of aspiration and frugality creates a number of imperatives for marketing strategies in China.

Shape the decision
Convincing consumers of the importance of your product (as it applies to job success or status, for example) will increase your ability to channel trade-up spending. A strong Web site with a consumer education tilt is key, as are highly skilled in-store sales people who know your products.

Consumers in China who traded up to higher-quality goods traded down in a larger number of categories.

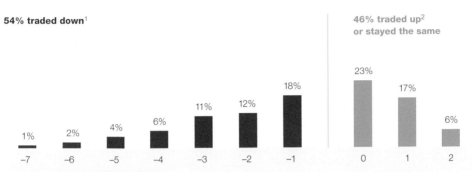

54% traded down[1]

46% traded up[2] or stayed the same

1% 2% 4% 6% 11% 12% 18% 23% 17% 6%

−7 −6 −5 −4 −3 −2 −1 0 1 2

Net number of categories traded
(for example, a consumer who traded up in 5 categories and traded down in 7 is counted in the −2 column)

[1] Traded down: either bought the same amount of a particular product, but at a lower quality and price, or purchased less of the product at the same quality and price.
[2] Traded up: bought the same amount of a particular product but at a higher quality and price.

Source: 2010 McKinsey annual survey of Chinese consumers

Identify cross-promotion opportunities

Decisions to trade up aren't made in isolation. Consumers who upgrade their choice of an entertainment venue, for example, are also likely to upgrade their choice of alcohol, creating opportunities for spirits vendors to partner with trendy bars and restaurants.

Rethink low-cost, low-quality strategies

Companies that have relied on down-market business models to win Chinese spenders may find themselves on the losing end of trade-up, trade-off choices. ○

[1] Yuval Atsmon et al., "2010 Annual Chinese Consumer Study: Trading up or trading off? Chinese consumers become increasingly pragmatic," McKinsey Insights China, August 2010.

The authors would like to acknowledge Vinay Dixit, Glenn Leibowitz, Anita Ngai, Ian St-Maurice, Vera Tang, Cherie Zhang, and Rachel Zheng for their contributions to this article.

Yuval Atsmon and **Max Magni** are principals in McKinsey's Shanghai office.

For a broader discussion of China's consumers, see "China's new pragmatic consumers," on mckinseyquarterly.com.

A better way to anticipate downturns

Tim Koller

Credit markets, though harder to follow than equity markets, provide a clearer warning when economic decline looms.

The daily barrage of conflicting economic reports provides executives with few reliable clues about whether the global recovery will be durable or, instead, lapse into another bout of recession. In response, many leaders fixate on movements in equity markets as augurs of future conditions that will shape key business decisions.[1] They shouldn't. McKinsey research shows that stock markets are notably poor predictors of downturns and that credit markets are a much better indicator of where trouble may be brewing, since they often lie at the center of financial crises and recessions. While parsing the credit markets isn't easy—there's no dominant indicator of market direction, such as the Dow Jones industrial average—executives who take the time to understand credit market patterns will be better prepared when future crises arrive.

Canaries in the coal mine
During every major recession since the early 1970s, most of the decline in the S&P 500 index occurred after the economy had already slowed. Equity markets missed the boat by giving too much weight to current rather than future eco-

nomic activity. Moreover, when equity values have dropped during nonrecessionary periods, that has rarely signaled looming economic distress.

Unlike equity markets, credit markets often start to fray as difficult times begin. Indeed, they drive most downturns—crises incubate there before radiating through the real economy.

There are several reasons for this phenomenon. Credit markets often suffer from chronic groupthink, as most banks and other financial players follow the same investing and trading strategies. These markets also are extremely illiquid compared with stock markets, making it difficult for investors with contrarian views to apply them. Expectations of government bailouts create a tremendous moral hazard that expands the terrain of these risky strategies and makes it impossible for the market to correct itself. Finally, when things go wrong, they often go very wrong indeed: credit evaporates, triggering distressed-asset sales.

Signs of stress

Executives feeling a measure of optimism given today's relatively buoyant equity markets should also pay heed to the more somber credit picture, which reveals continuing uncertainty in formerly overheated real-estate markets. The government now dominates them, and the owners of at least five million houses are delinquent or in foreclosure—with an uncertain ultimate resolution, leaving many banks vulnerable. Meanwhile, levels of government debt in the United States and elsewhere are problematic and rising.[2] Since the conditions for a crisis are typically in place several years before it becomes visible, such stresses merit careful monitoring, as do some common early-warning signs.

Loose lending standards

One clear sign of trouble ahead is a deterioration of lending criteria. In the late 1980s, for instance, banks issued debt based on wildly optimistic assumptions of earnings growth, even for industries in long-term decline. And during the 2005 US real-estate bubble, buyers could purchase a house with little or no evidence of their ability to carry a mortgage.

Unusually high leverage

Another warning signal is unusually high debt levels. In the months leading up to the real-estate crisis in

Most of the decline in equity markets comes after a recession has already begun.

S&P 500

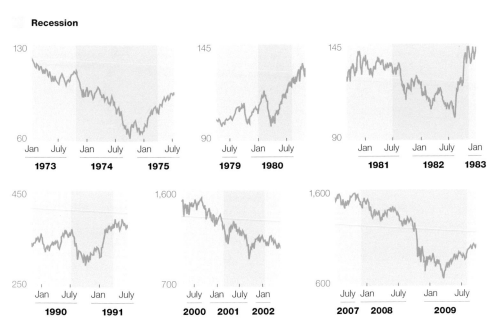

Source: S&P 500; McKinsey analysis

Stock market declines do not indicate economic downturns.

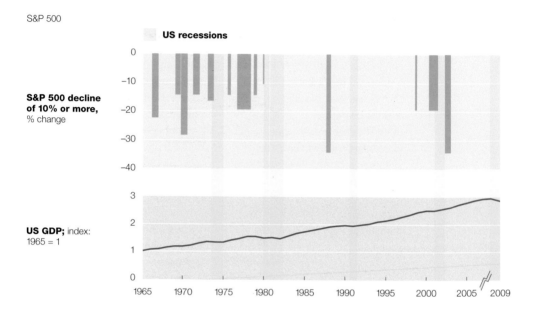

S&P 500

US recessions

S&P 500 decline of 10% or more, % change

US GDP; index: 1965 = 1

Most major downturns in the past 30 to 40 years have been driven by some sort of credit crisis.

	Crisis	Start date	Real GDP change after crisis, %
US crisis	Federal Reserve Board inflation crackdown	1980	−2
	Savings-and-loan, junk bond crisis	1990	0
	US subprime-mortgage crisis	Dec 2007	−2
Non-US crisis	Latin America (Mexico) debt crisis	1982	−4
	Japan property market burst	1990	3
	Mexico debt crisis	Dec 1994	−6
	Asia (Thailand) debt crisis	July 1997	−11
	Russia default	Aug 1998	−5
	Argentina economic crisis	1999	−1
	Greek/eurozone crisis	Dec 2009	N/A

2007, both banks and consumers in the United States were exceptionally highly leveraged. Hedge funds were another, albeit obscure, factor: although the general public had no visibility into how leveraged they were, the banks lending to them did—yet no single bank was willing to give up this profitable business.

Transactions without value

Subtle signs that are difficult for casual observers to notice often indicate that financial transactions are proliferating even when they aren't creating value. Many collateralized debt obligations, the instruments that gave rise to the credit crisis, fall into this category. Whenever a company uses oblique methods to take debt off its balance sheet, investors would be well advised to wonder why. These transactions generate a lot of fees for bankers but rarely create any value.

•   •   •

Executives with the tenacity to follow issues like these, along with the many other moving parts of the credit markets, will be more likely than those who focus on the equity markets to adjust strategies in order to deal with economic disarray before it strikes. ○

[1] Executives in our global survey are evenly split on where the economy is headed. See "Economic Conditions Snapshot, September 2010: McKinsey Global Survey results," mckinseyquarterly.com, September 2010.

[2] Indeed, US industrial companies that entered the crisis with healthy balance sheets withstood it reasonably well precisely because these companies were not overleveraged and had sufficient cash reserves to be flexible as it wore on.

Tim Koller is a principal in McKinsey's New York office.

The full version of this article is available on mckinseyquarterly.com.

Test for bad strategy

Do you have a strategy—crisp thinking about how to concentrate your resources to gain a competitive edge? Or are you stuck with piles of planning documents and fluffy, amorphous goals? The articles in this package will help you decide. Learn from Richard Rumelt about how pervasive "bad strategy" can be. Then dig into ten timeless tests of strategy that leading thinkers from McKinsey are using to stimulate strategic dialogue in corporations around the world. Finally, ponder the tough questions that senior executives in the trenches have asked about their strategies.

Artwork by Neil Webb

The perils of bad strategy

Richard Rumelt

Bad strategy abounds, says UCLA
management professor Richard Rumelt.
Senior executives who can spot it
stand a much better chance of creating
good strategies.

Horatio Nelson had a problem. The British admiral's fleet was
outnumbered at Trafalgar by an armada of French and Spanish ships
that Napoleon had ordered to disrupt Britain's commerce and prepare for a cross-channel invasion. The prevailing tactics in 1805 were
for the two opposing fleets to stay in line, firing broadsides at each
other. But Nelson had a strategic insight into how to deal with being
outnumbered. He broke the British fleet into two columns and drove
them at the Franco-Spanish fleet, hitting its line perpendicularly. The
lead British ships took a great risk, but Nelson judged that the less-
trained Franco-Spanish gunners would not be able to compensate for
the heavy swell that day and that the enemy fleet, with its coherence
lost, would be no match for the more experienced British captains and
gunners in the ensuing melee. He was proved right: the French and
Spanish lost 22 ships, two-thirds of their fleet. The British lost none.[1]

Nelson's victory is a classic example of good strategy, which almost
always looks this simple and obvious in retrospect. It does not pop out
of some strategic-management tool, matrix, triangle, or fill-in-the-
blanks scheme. Instead, a talented leader has identified the one or two
critical issues in a situation—the pivot points that can multiply the
effectiveness of effort—and then focused and concentrated action and
resources on them. A good strategy does more than urge us forward

[1] Nelson himself was mortally wounded at Trafalgar, becoming, in death, Britain's greatest
naval hero. The battle ensured Britain's naval dominance, which remained secure for a
century and a half.

This article is adapted from Richard Rumelt's *Good Strategy/ Bad Strategy: The Difference and Why It Matters*, to be published in July 2011 by Crown Publishing.

toward a goal or vision; it honestly acknowledges the challenges we face and provides an approach to overcoming them.

Too many organizational leaders say they have a strategy when they do not. Instead, they espouse what I call "bad strategy." Bad strategy ignores the power of choice and focus, trying instead to accommodate a multitude of conflicting demands and interests. Like a quarterback whose only advice to his teammates is "let's win," bad strategy covers up its failure to guide by embracing the language of broad goals, ambition, vision, and values. Each of these elements is, of course, an important part of human life. But, by themselves, they are not substitutes for the hard work of strategy.

In this article, I try to lay out the attributes of bad strategy and explain why it is so prevalent. Make no mistake: the creeping spread of bad strategy affects us all. Heavy with goals and slogans, governments have become less and less able to solve problems. Corporate boards sign off on strategic plans that are little more than wishful thinking. The US education system is rich with targets and standards but poor at comprehending and countering the sources of underperformance. The only remedy is for us to demand more from those who lead. More than charisma and vision, we must demand good strategy.

The hallmarks of bad strategy

I coined the term bad strategy in 2007 at a Washington, DC, seminar on national-security strategy. My role was to provide a business and corporate-strategy perspective. The participants expected, I think, that my remarks would detail the seriousness and growing competence with which business strategy was created. Using words and slides, I told the group that many businesses did have powerful, effective strategies. But in my personal experiences with corporate practice, I saw a growing profusion of bad strategy.

In the years since that seminar, I have had the opportunity to discuss the bad-strategy concept with a number of senior executives. In the process, I have condensed my list of its key hallmarks to four points: the failure to face the challenge, mistaking goals for strategy, bad strategic objectives, and fluff.

Failure to face the problem

A strategy is a way through a difficulty, an approach to overcoming an obstacle, a response to a challenge. If the challenge is not defined, it is difficult or impossible to assess the quality of the strategy. And, if you cannot assess that, you cannot reject a bad strategy or improve a good one.

International Harvester learned about this element of bad strategy the hard way. In July 1979, the company's strategic and financial planners produced a thick sheaf of paper titled "Corporate Strategic Plan: International Harvester." It was an amalgam of five separate strategic plans, each created by one of the operating divisions.

The strategic plan did not lack for texture and detail. Looking, for example, within the agricultural-equipment group—International Harvester's core, dating back to the McCormick reaper, which was a foundation of the company—there is information and discussion about each segment. The overall intent was to strengthen the dealer/distributor network and to reduce manufacturing costs. Market share in agricultural equipment was also projected to increase, from 16 percent to 20 percent.

The 'great pushes' during World War I led to the deaths of a generation of European youths. Maybe that's why motivational speakers are not the staple on the European management-lecture circuit that they are in the United States.

That was typical of the overall strategy, which was to increase the company's share in each market, cut costs in each business, and thereby ramp up revenue and profit. A summary graph, showing past and forecast profit, forms an almost perfect hockey stick, with an immediate recovery from decline followed by a steady rise.

The problem with all this was that the plan didn't even mention Harvester's grossly inefficient production facilities, especially in its agricultural-equipment business, or the fact that Harvester had the *worst* labor relations in US industry. As a result, the company's profit margin had been about one-half of its competitors' for a long time. As a corporation, International Harvester's main problem was its inefficient work organization—a problem that would not be solved by investing in new equipment or pressing managers to increase market share.

By cutting administrative overhead, Harvester boosted reported profits for a year or two. But following a disastrous six-month strike, the company quickly began to collapse. It sold off various businesses—including its agricultural-equipment business, to Tenneco. The truck division, renamed Navistar, is today a leading maker of heavy trucks and engines.

To summarize: if you fail to identify and analyze the obstacles, you don't have a strategy. Instead, you have a stretch goal or a budget or a list of things you wish would happen.

Mistaking goals for strategy

A few years ago, a CEO I'll call Chad Logan asked me to work with the management team of his graphic-arts company on "strategic thinking." Logan explained that his overall goal was simple—he called it the "20/20 plan." Revenues were to grow at 20 percent a year, and the profit margin was to be 20 percent or higher.

"This 20/20 plan is a very aggressive financial goal," I said. "What has to happen for it to be realized?" Logan tapped the plan with a blunt forefinger. "The thing I learned as a football player is that winning requires strength and skill, but more than anything it requires the will to win—the drive to succeed. . . . Sure, 20/20 is a stretch, but the secret of success is setting your sights high. We are going to keep pushing until we get there."

I tried again: "Chad, when a company makes the kind of jump in performance your plan envisions, there is usually a key strength you are building on or a change in the industry that opens up new opportunities. Can you clarify what the point of leverage might be here, in your company?"

Logan frowned and pressed his lips together, expressing frustration that I didn't understand him. He pulled a sheet of paper out of his briefcase and ran a finger under the highlighted text. "This is what Jack Welch says," he told me. The text read: "We have found that by reaching for what appears to be the impossible, we often actually do the impossible." (Logan's reading of Welch was, of course, highly selective. Yes, Welch believed in stretch goals. But he also said, "If you don't have a competitive advantage, don't compete.")

The reference to "pushing until we get there" triggered in my mind an association with the great pushes of 1915–17 during World War I, which led to the deaths of a generation of European youths. Maybe that's why motivational speakers are not the staple on the European management-lecture circuit that they are in the United States. For the slaughtered troops did not suffer from a lack of motivation. They suffered from a lack of competent strategic leadership. A leader may justly ask for "one last push," but the leader's job is more than that. The job of the leader—the strategist—is also to create the conditions that will make the push effective, to have a strategy worthy of the effort called upon.

Bad strategic objectives

Another sign of bad strategy is fuzzy strategic objectives. One form this problem can take is a scrambled mess of things to accomplish—a dog's dinner of goals. A long list of things to do, often mislabeled as strategies or objectives, is not a strategy. It is just a list of things to do. Such lists usually grow out of planning meetings in which a wide variety of stakeholders suggest things they would like to see accomplished. Rather than focus on a few important items, the group sweeps the whole day's collection into the strategic plan. Then, in recognition that it is a dog's dinner, the label "long term" is added, implying that none of these things need be done today. As a vivid example, I recently had the chance to discuss strategy with the mayor of a small city in the Pacific Northwest. His planning committee's strategic plan contained 47 strategies and 178 action items. Action item number 122 was "create a strategic plan."

A second type of weak strategic objective is one that is "blue sky"— typically a simple restatement of the desired state of affairs or of the challenge. It skips over the annoying fact that no one has a clue as to how to get there. A leader may successfully identify the key challenge and propose an overall approach to dealing with the challenge. But if the consequent strategic objectives are just as difficult to meet as the original challenge, the strategy has added little value.

Good strategy, in contrast, works by focusing energy and resources on one, or a very few, pivotal objectives whose accomplishment will lead to a cascade of favorable outcomes. It also builds a bridge between the critical challenge at the heart of the strategy and action—between desire and immediate objectives that lie within grasp. Thus, the objectives that a good strategy sets stand a good chance of being accomplished, given existing resources and competencies.

Fluff

A final hallmark of mediocrity and bad strategy is superficial abstraction—a flurry of fluff—designed to mask the absence of thought.

Fluff is a restatement of the obvious, combined with a generous sprinkling of buzzwords that masquerade as expertise. Here is a quote from a major retail bank's internal strategy memoranda: "Our fundamental strategy is one of customer-centric intermediation." Intermediation means that the company accepts deposits and then lends out the money. In other words, it is a bank. The buzzphrase "customer centric" could mean that the bank competes by offering better terms and service, but an examination of its policies does not reveal any distinction in this regard. The phrase "customer-centric intermediation" is pure fluff. Remove the fluff and you learn that the bank's fundamental strategy is being a bank.

Why so much bad strategy?

Bad strategy has many roots, but I'll focus on two here: the inability to choose and template-style planning—filling in the blanks with "vision, mission, values, strategies."

The inability to choose

Strategy involves focus and, therefore, choice. And choice means setting aside some goals in favor of others. When this hard work is not done, weak strategy is the result. In 1992, I sat in on a strategy discussion among senior executives at Digital Equipment Corporation (DEC). A leader of the minicomputer revolution of the 1960s and 1970s, DEC had been losing ground for several years to the newer 32-bit personal computers. There were serious doubts that the company could survive for long without dramatic changes.

To simplify matters, I will pretend that only three executives were present. "Alec" argued that DEC had always been a computer company and should continue integrating hardware and software into usable systems. "Beverly" felt that the only distinctive resource DEC had to build on was its customer relationships. Hence, she derided Alec's "Boxes" strategy and argued in favor of a "Solutions" strategy that solved customer problems. "Craig" held that the heart of the computer industry was semiconductor technology and that the company should focus its resources on designing and building better "Chips."

Choice was necessary: both the Chips and Solutions strategies represented dramatic transformations of the firm, and each would require wholly new skills and work practices. One wouldn't choose either risky alternative unless the status quo Boxes strategy was likely to fail. And one wouldn't choose to do both Chips and Solutions at the same

Scan through template-style planning documents and you will find pious statements of the obvious presented as if they were decisive insights.

time, because there was little common ground between them. It is not feasible to do two separate, deep transformations of a company's core at once.

With equally powerful executives arguing for each of the three conflicting strategies, the meeting was intense. DEC's chief executive, Ken Olsen, had made the mistake of asking the group to reach a consensus. It was unable to do that, because a majority preferred Solutions to Boxes, a majority preferred Boxes to Chips, and a majority also preferred Chips to Solutions. No matter which of the three paths was chosen, a majority preferred something else. This dilemma wasn't unique to the stand-off at DEC. The French philosopher Nicolas de Condorcet achieved immortality by first pointing out the possibility of such a paradox arising, and economist Kenneth Arrow won a Nobel Prize for showing that "Condorcet's paradox" cannot be resolved through cleverer voting schemes.

Not surprisingly, the group compromised on a statement: "DEC is committed to providing high-quality products and services and being a leader in data processing." This fluffy, amorphous statement was, of course, not a strategy. It was a political outcome reached by individuals who, forced to reach a consensus, could not agree on which interests and concepts to forego.

Ken Olsen was replaced, in June 1992, by Robert Palmer, who had headed the company's semiconductor engineering. Palmer made it clear that the strategy would be Chips. One point of view had finally won. But by then it was five years too late. Palmer stopped the losses for a while but could not stem the tide of ever more powerful personal computers that were overtaking the firm. In 1998, DEC was acquired by Compaq, which, in turn, was acquired by Hewlett-Packard three years later.

Template-style strategy

The Jack Welch quote about "reaching for what appears to be the impossible" is fairly standard motivational fare, available from literally hundreds of motivational speakers, books, calendars, memo pads, and Web sites. This fascination with positive thinking has helped inspire ideas about charismatic leadership and the power of a shared vision, reducing them to something of a formula. The general outline goes like this: the transformational leader (1) develops or has a vision, (2) inspires people to sacrifice (change) for the good of the organization, and (3) empowers people to accomplish the vision.

By the early 2000s, the juxtaposition of vision-led leadership and strategy work had produced a template-style system of strategic planning. (Type "vision mission strategy" into a search engine and you'll find thousands of examples of this kind of template for sale and in use.) The template looks like this:

The Vision. Fill in your vision of what the school/business/nation will be like in the future. Currently popular visions are to be the best or the leading or the best known.

The Mission. Fill in a high-sounding, politically correct statement of the purpose of the school/business/nation. Innovation, human progress, and sustainable solutions are popular elements of a mission statement.

The Values. Fill in a statement that describes the company's values. Make sure they are noncontroversial. Key words include "integrity," "respect," and "excellence."

The Strategies. Fill in some aspirations/goals but call them strategies. For example, "to invest in a portfolio of performance businesses that create value for our shareholders and growth for our customers."

This template-style planning has been enthusiastically adopted by corporations, school boards, university presidents, and government agencies. Scan through such documents and you will find pious statements of the obvious presented as if they were decisive insights. The enormous problem all this creates is that someone who actually wishes to conceive and implement an effective strategy is surrounded by empty rhetoric and bad examples.

The kernel of good strategy

By now, I hope you are fully awake to the dramatic differences between good and bad strategy. Let me close by trying to give you a leg up in crafting good strategies, which have a basic underlying structure:

1. A diagnosis: an explanation of the nature of the challenge. A good diagnosis simplifies the often overwhelming complexity of reality by identifying certain aspects of the situation as being the critical ones.

2. A guiding policy: an overall approach chosen to cope with or over-come the obstacles identified in the diagnosis.

3. Coherent actions: steps that are coordinated with one another to support the accomplishment of the guiding policy.

I'll illustrate by describing Nvidia's journey from troubled start-up to market leader for 3-D graphics chips. Nvidia's first product, a PC add-in board for video, audio, and 3-D graphics, was a commercial failure. In 1995, rival start-up 3Dfx Interactive took the lead in serving the burgeoning demand of gamers for fast 3-D graphics chips. Furthermore, there were rumors that industry giant Intel was thinking about introducing its own 3-D graphics chip. The diagnosis: "We are losing the performance race."

Nvidia CEO Jen-Hsun Huang's key insight was that given the rapid state of advance in 3-D graphics, releasing a new chip every 6 months—instead of at the industry-standard rate of every 18 months—would make a critical difference. The guiding policy, in short, was to "release a faster, better chip three times faster than the industry norm."

To accomplish this fast-release cycle, the company emphasized several coherent actions: it formed three development teams, which worked on overlapping schedules; it invested in massive simulation and emula-tion facilities to avoid delays in the fabrication of chips and in the development of software drivers; and, over time, it regained control of driver development from the branded add-in board makers.

Over the next decade, the strategy worked brilliantly. Intel introduced its 3-D graphics chip in 1998 but did not keep up the pace, exiting the business of discrete 3-D graphics chips a year later. In 2000, creditors of 3Dfx initiated bankruptcy proceedings against the company, which was struggling to keep up with Nvidia. In 2007, *Forbes* named Nvidia "Company of the Year."[2]

●   ●   ●

Despite the roar of voices equating strategy with ambition, leadership, vision, or planning, strategy is none of these. Rather, it is coherent action backed by an argument. And the core of the strategist's work is always the same: discover the crucial factors in a situation and design a way to coordinate and focus actions to deal with them. ○

[2] The effectiveness of even good strategies isn't permanently assured. ATI, now part of AMD, has become a powerful competitor in graphics processing units, and Nvidia has been challenged in the fast-growing mobile-graphics business, where cost is often more important than performance.

Richard Rumelt is the Harry and Elsa Kunin Professor of Business and Society at the UCLA Anderson School of Management.

Have you tested your strategy lately?

Chris Bradley, Martin Hirt, and Sven Smit

Ten timeless tests can help you kick the tires on your strategy and kick up the level of strategic dialogue throughout your company.

'What's the next new thing in strategy?' a senior executive recently asked Phil Rosenzweig, a professor at IMD,[1] in Switzerland. His response was surprising for someone whose career is devoted to advancing the state of the art of strategy: "With all respect, I think that's the wrong question. There's always new stuff out there, and most of it's not very good. Rather than looking for the next musing, it's probably better to be thorough about what we know is true and make sure we do that well."

Let's face it: the basic principles that make for good strategy often get obscured. Sometimes the explanation is a quest for the next new thing— natural in a field that emerged through the steady accumulation of frameworks promising to unlock the secret of competitive advantage.[2] In other cases, the culprit is torrents of data, reams of analysis, and piles of documents that can be more distracting than enlightening.

Ultimately, strategy is a way of thinking, not a procedural exercise or a set of frameworks. To stimulate that thinking and the dialogue that goes along with it, we developed a set of tests aimed at helping executives assess the strength of their strategies. We focused on testing the strategy itself (in other words, the output of the strategy-development process), rather than the frameworks, tools, and approaches that

[1] International Institute for Management Development.
[2] For a rich account of strategy's birth and growth as a field, see Walter Kiechel, *The Lords of Strategy*, Boston, MA: Harvard Business School Press, 2010.

Most companies' strategies pass fewer than four of the ten tests.

Number of tests rated as fully consistent with company strategy, % of respondents

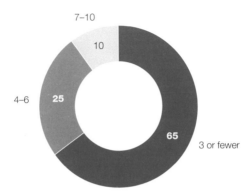

Source: 2010 McKinsey survey of 2,135 global executives on testing business strategy

generate strategies, for two reasons. First, companies develop strategy in many different ways, often idiosyncratic to their organizations, people, and markets. Second, many strategies emerge over time rather than from a process of deliberate formulation.[3]

There are ten tests on our list, and not all are created equal. The first—"will it beat the market?"—is comprehensive. The remaining nine disaggregate the picture of a market-beating strategy, though it's certainly possible for a strategy to succeed without "passing" all nine of them. This list may sound more complicated than the three Cs or the five forces of strategy.[4] But detailed pressure testing, in our experience, helps pinpoint more precisely where the strategy needs work, while generating a deeper and more fruitful strategic dialogue.

Those conversations matter, but they often are loose and disjointed. We heard that, loud and clear, over the past two years in workshops where we explored our tests with more than 700 senior strategists around the world. Furthermore, a recent *McKinsey Quarterly* survey

[3] For a classic statement of the idea that strategies are more emergent than planned, see Henry Mintzberg, "Crafting strategy," *Harvard Business Review*, 1987, July–August, Volume 65, Number 4, pp. 66–75.

[4] The three Cs and the five forces are seminal strategy frameworks. The three Cs (competitors, customers, and company) were articulated by retired McKinsey partner Kenichi Ohmae in *The Mind of the Strategist* (McGraw-Hill, 1982). The five forces (barriers to entry, buyer power, supplier power, the threat of substitutes, and the degree of rivalry) were set forth by Harvard Business School professor Michael Porter in *Competitive Strategy* (Free Press, 1998).

of 2,135 executives indicates that few strategies pass more than three of the tests. In contrast, the reflections of a range of current and former strategy practitioners (see "How we do it: Strategic tests from four senior executives," on page 54) suggest that the tests described here help formalize something that the best strategists do quite intuitively.

The tests of a good strategy are timeless in nature. But the ability to pressure-test a strategy is especially timely now. The financial crisis of 2008 and the recession that followed made some strategies obsolete, revealed weaknesses in others, and forced many companies to confront choices and trade-offs they put off in boom years. At the same time, a shift toward shorter planning cycles and decentralized strategic decision making are increasing the utility of a common set of tests.[5] All this makes today an ideal time to kick the tires on your strategy.

Test 1:

Will your strategy beat the market?

All companies operate in markets surrounded by customers, suppliers, competitors, substitutes, and potential entrants, all seeking to advance their own positions. That process, unimpeded, inexorably drives economic surplus—the gap between the return a company earns and its cost of capital—toward zero.

For a company to beat the market by capturing and retaining an economic surplus, there must be an imperfection that stops or at least slows the working of the market. An imperfection controlled by a company is a competitive advantage. These are by definition scarce and fleeting because markets drive reversion to mean performance. The best companies are emulated by those in the middle of the pack, and the worst exit or undergo significant reform. As each player responds to and learns from the actions of others, best practice becomes commonplace rather than a market-beating strategy. Good strategies emphasize difference—versus your direct competitors, versus potential substitutes, and versus potential entrants.

Market participants play out the drama of competition on a stage beset by randomness. Because the evolution of markets is path dependent—that is, its current state at any one time is the sum product of all pre-

[5] For more on strategy setting in today's environment, see Lowell Bryan, "Dynamic management: Better decisions in uncertain times," mckinseyquarterly.com, December 2009; and "Navigating the new normal: A conversation with four chief strategy officers," mckinseyquarterly.com, December 2009.

Markets drive a reversion to mean performance.

Performance cohorts based on position in 2001 relative to mean, n = 743[1]

Top quintile
Middle quintile
Bottom quintile

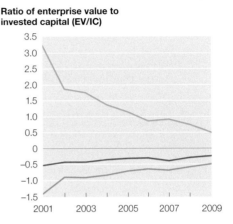

Return on invested
capital (ROIC), %

Ratio of enterprise value to
invested capital (EV/IC)

[1] Sample of largest 1,200 nonfinancial US-listed companies in 2009 was narrowed to 743 that were also listed in 2001.
Source: Standard & Poor's Compustat; McKinsey analysis

vious events, including a great many random ones—the winners of today are often the accidents of history. Consider the development of the US tire industry. At its peak in the mid-1920s, a frenzy of entry had created almost 300 competitors. Yet by the 1940s, four producers controlled more than 70 percent of the market. Those winners happened to make retrospectively lucky choices about location and technology, but at the time it was difficult to tell which companies were truly fit for the evolving environment. The histories of many other industries, from aerospace to information technology, show remarkably similar patterns.

To beat the market, therefore, advantages have to be robust and responsive in the face of onrushing market forces. Few companies, in our experience, ask themselves if they are beating the market—the pressures of "just playing along" seem intense enough. But playing along can feel safer than it is. Weaker contenders win surprisingly often in war when they deploy a divergent strategy, and the same is true in business.[6]

[6] See Ivan Arreguin-Toft, *How the weak win wars: A theory of asymmetric conflict*, Cambridge, UK: Cambridge University Press, 2005.

Test 2:

Does your strategy tap a true source of advantage?

Know your competitive advantage, and you've answered the question of why you make money (and vice versa). Competitive advantage stems from two sources of scarcity: positional advantages and special capabilities.

Positional advantages are rooted in structurally attractive markets. By definition, such advantages favor incumbents: they create an asymmetry between those inside and those outside high walls. For example, in Australia, two beer makers control 95 percent of the market and enjoy triple the margins of US brewers. This situation has sustained itself for two decades, but it wasn't always so. Beginning in the 1980s, the Australian industry experienced consolidation. That change in structure was associated with a change in industry conduct (price growth began outstripping general inflation) and a change in industry performance (higher profitability). Understanding the relationship among structure, conduct, and performance is a critical part of the quest for positional advantage.

Special capabilities, the second source of competitive advantage, are scarce resources whose possession confers unique benefits. The most obvious resources, such as drug patents or leases on mineral deposits, we call "privileged, tradable assets": they can be bought and sold. A second category of special capabilities, "distinctive competencies," consists of things a company does particularly well, such as innovating or managing stakeholders. These capabilities can be just as powerful in creating advantage but cannot be easily traded.

Too often, companies are cavalier about claiming special capabilities. Such a capability must be critical to a company's profits and exist in abundance within it while being scarce outside. As such, special capabilities tend to be specific in nature and few in number. Companies often err here by mistaking size for scale advantage or overestimating their ability to leverage capabilities across markets. They infer special capabilities from observed performance, often without considering other explanations (such as luck or positional advantage). Companies should test any claimed capability advantage vigorously before pinning their hopes on it.

When companies bundle together activities that collectively create advantage, it becomes more difficult for competitors to identify and replicate its exact source. Consider Aldi, the highly successful discount grocery retailer. To deliver its value proposition of lower prices, Aldi has completely redesigned the typical business system of a supermarket: only 1,500 or so products rather than 30,000, the stocking of one own-brand or private label rather than hundreds of national brands, and superlean replenishment on pallets and trolleys, thus avoiding the expensive task of hand stacking shelves. Given the enormous changes necessary for any supermarket that wishes to copy the total system, it is extremely difficult to mimic Aldi's value proposition.

Finally, don't forget to take a dynamic view. What can erode positional advantage? Which special capabilities are becoming vulnerable? There is every reason to believe that competitors will exploit points of vulnerability. Assume, like Lewis Carroll's Red Queen, that you have to run just to stay in the same place.

Test 3: Is your strategy granular about where to compete?

The need to beat the market begs the question of which market. Research shows that the unit of analysis used in determining strategy (essentially, the degree to which a market is segmented) significantly influences resource allocation and thus the likelihood of success: dividing the same businesses in different ways leads to strikingly different capital allocations.

What is the right level of granularity? Push within reason for the finest possible objective segmentation of the market: think 30 to 50 segments rather than the more typical 5 or so. Too often, by contrast, the business unit as defined by the organizational chart becomes the default for defining markets, reducing from the start the potential scope of strategic thinking.

Defining and understanding these segments correctly is one of the most practical things a company can do to improve its strategy. Management at one large bank attributed fast growth and share gains to measurably superior customer perceptions and satisfaction. Examining the bank's markets at a more granular level suggested that 90 percent of its outperformance could be attributed to a relatively high exposure to one fast-growing city and to a presence in a fast-growing product segment. This insight helped the bank avoid building its strategy on false assumptions about what was and wasn't working for the operation as a whole.

In fact, 80 percent of the variance in revenue growth is explained by choices about where to compete, according to research summarized in *The Granularity of Growth*,[7] leaving only 20 percent explained by choices about how to compete. Unfortunately, this is the exact opposite of the allocation of time and effort in a typical strategy-development process. Companies should be shifting their attention greatly toward the "where" and should strive to outposition competitors by regularly reallocating resources as opportunities shift within and between segments.

Test 4: Does your strategy put you ahead of trends?

The emergence of new trends is the norm. But many strategies place too much weight on the continuation of the status quo because they extrapolate from the past three to five years, a time frame too brief to capture the true violence of market forces.

A major innovation or an external shock in regulation, demand, or technology, for example, can drive a rapid, full-scale industry transition. But most trends emerge fairly slowly—so slowly that companies generally fail to respond until a trend hits profits. At this point, it is too late to mount a strategically effective response, let alone shape the change to your advantage. Managers typically delay action, held back by sunk costs, an unwillingness to cannibalize a legacy business, or an attachment to yesterday's formula for success. The cost of delay is steep: consider the plight of major travel agency chains slow to understand the power of online intermediaries. Conversely, for companies that get ahead of the curve, major market transitions are an opportunity to rethink their commitments in areas ranging from technology to distribution and to tailor their strategies to the new environment.

To do so, strategists must take trend analysis seriously. Always look to the edges. How are early adopters and that small cadre of consumers who seem to be ahead of the curve acting? What are small, innovative entrants doing? What technologies under development could change the game? To see which trends really matter, assess their potential

---

[7] Mehrdad Baghai, Sven Smit, and Patrick Viguerie, *The Granularity of Growth: How to Identify the Sources of Growth and Drive Enduring Company Performance*, Hoboken, NJ: Wiley & Sons, 2008.

impact on the financial position of your company and articulate the decisions you would make differently if that outcome were certain. For example, don't just stop at an aging population as a trend—work it through to its conclusion. Which consumer behaviors would change? Which particular product lines would be affected? What would be the precise effect on the P&L? And how does that picture line up with today's investment priorities?

Test 5: Does your strategy rest on privileged insights?

Data today can be cheap, accessible, and easily assembled into detailed analyses that leave executives with the comfortable feeling of possessing an informed strategy. But much of this is noise and most of it is widely available to rivals. Furthermore, routinely analyzing readily available data diverts attention from where insight-creating advantage lies: in the weak signals buried in the noise.

In the 1990s, when the ability to burn music onto CDs emerged, no one knew how digitization would play out; MP3s, peer-to-peer file sharing, and streaming Web-based media were not on the horizon. But one corporation with a large record label recognized more rapidly than others that the practical advantage of copyright protection could quickly become diluted if consumers began copying material. Early recognition of that possibility allowed the CEO to sell the business at a multiple based on everyone else's assumption that the status quo was unthreatened.

Developing proprietary insights isn't easy. In fact, this is the element of good strategy where most companies stumble (see "The insight deficit," on page 124). A search for problems can help you get started. Create a short list of questions whose answers would have major implications for the company's strategy—for example, "What will we regret doing if the development of India hiccups or stalls, and what will we not regret?" In doing so, don't forget to examine the assumptions, explicit and implicit, behind an established business model. Do they still fit the current environment?

Another key is to collect new data through field observations or research rather than to recycle the same industry reports everyone else uses. Similarly, seeking novel ways to analyze the data can generate powerful new insights. For example, one supermarket chain we know recently rethought its store network strategy on the basis of surprising results from a new clustering algorithm.

Finally, many strategic breakthroughs have their root in a simple but profound customer insight (usually solving an old problem for the customer in a new way). In our experience, companies that go out of their way to experience the world from the customer's perspective routinely develop better strategies.

Test 6:

Does your strategy embrace uncertainty?

A central challenge of strategy is that we have to make choices now, but the payoffs occur in a future environment we cannot fully know or control. A critical step in embracing uncertainty is to try to characterize exactly what variety of it you face—a surprisingly rare activity at many companies. Our work over the years has emphasized four levels of uncertainty. Level one offers a reasonably clear view of the future: a range of outcomes tight enough to support a firm decision. At level two, there are a number of identifiable outcomes for which a company should prepare. At level three, the possible outcomes are represented not by a set of points but by a range that can be understood as a probability distribution. Level four features total ambiguity, where even the distribution of outcomes is unknown.

In our experience, companies oscillate between assuming, simplistically, that they are operating at level one (and making bold but unjustified point forecasts) and succumbing to an unnecessarily pessimistic level-four paralysis. In each case, careful analysis of the situation usually redistributes the variables into the middle ground of levels two and three.

Rigorously understanding the uncertainty you face starts with listing the variables that would influence a strategic decision and prioritizing them according to their impact. Focus early analysis on removing as much uncertainty as you can—by, for example, ruling out impossible outcomes and using the underlying economics at work to highlight outcomes that are either mutually reinforcing or unlikely because they would undermine one another in the market. Then apply tools such as scenario analysis to the remaining, irreducible uncertainty, which should be at the heart of your strategy.

Test 7:

Does your strategy balance commitment and flexibility?

Commitment and flexibility exist in inverse proportion to each other: the greater the commitment you make, the less flexibility remains. This tension is one of the core challenges of strategy. Indeed, strategy can be expressed as making the right trade-offs over time between commitment and flexibility.

Making such trade-offs effectively requires an understanding of which decisions involve commitment. Inside any large company, hundreds of people make thousands of decisions each year. Only a few are strategic: those that involve commitment through hard-to-reverse investments in long-lasting, company-specific assets. Commitment is the only path to sustainable competitive advantage.

In a world of uncertainty, strategy is about not just where and how to compete but also when. Committing too early can be a leap in the dark. Being too late is also dangerous, either because opportunities are perishable or rivals can seize advantage while your company stands on the sidelines. Flexibility is the essential ingredient that allows companies to make commitments when the risk/return trade-off seems most advantageous.

A market-beating strategy will focus on just a few crucial, high-commitment choices to be made now, while leaving flexibility for other such choices to be made over time. In practice, this approach means building your strategy as a portfolio comprising three things: big bets, or committed positions aimed at gaining significant competitive advantage; no-regrets moves, which will pay off whatever happens; and real options, or actions that involve relatively low costs now but can be elevated to a higher level of commitment as changing conditions warrant. You can build underpriced options into a strategy by, for example, modularizing major capital projects or maintaining the flexibility to switch between different inputs.

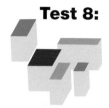

Test 8:   Is your strategy contaminated by bias?

It's possible to believe honestly that you have a market-beating strategy when, in fact, you don't. Sometimes, that's because forces beyond your control change. But in other cases, the cause is unintentional fuzzy thinking.

Behavioral economists have identified many characteristics of the brain that are often strengths in our broader, personal environment but that can work against us in the world of business decision making. The worst offenders include overoptimism (our tendency to hope for the best and believe too much in our own forecasts and abilities), anchoring (tying our valuation of something to an arbitrary reference point), loss aversion (putting too much emphasis on avoiding downsides and so eschewing risks worth taking), the confirmation bias (overweighting information that validates our opinions), herding (taking comfort in following the crowd), and the champion bias (assigning to an idea merit that's based on the person proposing it).

Strategy is especially prone to faulty logic because it relies on extrapolating ways to win in the future from a complex set of factors observed today. This is fertile ground for two big inference problems: attribution error (succumbing to the "halo effect") and survivorship bias (ignoring the "graveyard of silent failures"). Attribution error is the false attribution of success to observed factors; it is strategy by hindsight and assumes that replicating the actions of another company will lead to similar results. Survivorship bias refers to an analysis based on a surviving population, without consideration of those who

did not live to tell their tale: this approach skews our view of what caused success and presents no insights into what might cause failure—were the survivors just luckier? Case studies have their place, but hindsight is in reality not 20/20. There are too many unseen factors.

Developing multiple hypotheses and potential solutions to choose among is one way to "de-bias" decision making. Too often, the typical drill is to develop a promising hypothesis and put a lot of effort into building a fact base to validate it. In contrast, it is critical to bring fresh eyes to the issues and to maintain a culture of challenge, in which the obligation to dissent is fostered.

The decision-making process can also be de-biased by, for example, specifying objective decision criteria in advance and examining the possibility of being wrong. Techniques such as the "premortem assessment" (imagining yourself in a future where your decision turns out to have been mistaken and identifying why that might have been so) can also be useful.

Test 9: Is there conviction to act on your strategy?

This test and the one that follows aren't strictly about the strategy itself but about the investment you've made in implementing it—a distinction that in our experience quickly becomes meaningless because the two, inevitably, become intertwined. Many good strategies fall short in implementation because of an absence of conviction in the organization, particularly among the top team, where just one or two non-believers can strangle strategic change at birth.

Where a change of strategy is needed, that is usually because changes in the external environment have rendered obsolete the assumptions underlying a company's earlier strategy. To move ahead with implementation, you need a process that openly questions the old assumptions and allows managers to develop a new set of beliefs in tune with the new situation. This goal is not likely to be achieved just via lengthy reports and presentations. Nor will the social processes required to absorb new beliefs—group formation, building shared meaning, exposing and reconciling differences, aligning and accepting accountability—occur in formal meetings.

CEOs and boards should not be fooled by the warm glow they feel after a nice presentation by management. They must make sure that the whole team actually shares the new beliefs that support the strategy. This requirement means taking decision makers on a journey of discovery by creating experiences that will help them viscerally grasp mismatches that may exist between what the new strategy requires and the actions and behavior that have brought them success for many years. For example, visit plants and customers or tour a country your company plans to enter, so that the leadership team can personally meet crucial stakeholders. Mock-ups, video clips, and virtual experiences also can help.

The result of such an effort should be a support base of influencers who feel connected to the strategy and may even become evangelists for it. Because strategy often emanates from the top, and CEOs are accustomed to being heeded, this commonsense step often gets overlooked, to the great detriment of the strategy.

Test 10: Have you translated your strategy into an action plan?

In implementing any new strategy, it's imperative to define clearly what you are moving *from* and where you are moving *to* with respect to your company's business model, organization, and capabilities. Develop a detailed view of the shifts required to make the move, and ensure that processes and mechanisms, for which individual executives must be accountable, are in place to effect the changes. Quite simply, this is an action plan. Everyone needs to know what to do. Be sure that each major "from–to shift" is matched with the energy to make it happen. And since the totality of the change often represents a major organizational transformation, make sure you and your senior team are drawing on the large body of research and experience offering solid advice on change management—a topic beyond the scope of this article!

Finally, don't forget to make sure your ongoing resource allocation processes are aligned with your strategy. If you want to know what it actually is, look where the best people and the most generous budgets are—and be prepared to change these things significantly. Effort spent aligning the budget with the strategy will pay off many times over.

•   •   •

As we've discussed the tests with hundreds of senior executives at many of the world's largest companies, we've come away convinced that a lot of these topics are part of the strategic dialogue in organizations. But we've also heard time and again that discussion of such issues is often, as one executive in Japan recently told us, "random, simultaneous, and extremely confusing." Our hope is that the tests will prove a simple and effective antidote: a means of quickly identifying gaps in executives' strategic thinking, opening their minds toward new ways of using strategy to create value, and improving the quality of the strategy-development process itself. ○

The authors wish to acknowledge the many contributions of McKinsey alumnus Nick Percy, now the head of strategy for BBC Worldwide, to the thinking behind this article.

Chris Bradley is a principal in McKinsey's Sydney office, **Martin Hirt** is a director in the Taipei office, and **Sven Smit** is a director in the Amsterdam office.

Dig deeper on mckinseyquarterly.com by reading the article and related thinking on each of the ten tests, as well as detailed survey results.

How we do it:

Strategic tests from four senior executives

Raymond Gilmartin,
former CEO of Merck

Gail Lumsden,
group head of strategy
and planning at SABMiller

David Speiser,
senior vice president
for strategy at SAIC

Jeffrey Elton,
CEO and vice chairman
of KEW Group

All strategists grapple with the question of how to create and
preserve competitive advantage. But individual perspectives are
likely to differ, depending on a company's strategic journey, the industry it's in, and the idiosyncrasies of the organization. We talked
with four current or former senior strategists from diverse corporate
environments and markets about their strategic challenges—and
came away with four distinct, thought-provoking lists of strategic tests.

Raymond Gilmartin

Raymond Gilmartin, a professor at Harvard Business School and
a member of the board of directors at General Mills and
Microsoft, was the CEO of pharmaceutical company Merck from
1994 until 2005.

Does it violate any strategic laws of gravity?
I have been interested in strategy, both at a conceptual level and as
a practitioner, since the late 1960s, when I was studying at the Harvard
Business School and the transition was under way from talking about
long-range planning to thinking about strategy. At that time, many core
conceptual frameworks of strategy were emerging.

Having been exposed to these strategic frameworks early in my career, and believing there were certain principles that one should follow in formulating strategy, a test that I found useful was to look for situations where these principles were violated. For example, if you've got a 5 percent market share and somebody else in the industry has 40 percent, the idea that you're going to make dramatic gains in market share within a relatively short period of time is just unrealistic. Equally unrealistic is wanting to introduce a product that's undifferentiated and expecting to gain market share just because it's a big market.

I'm using very simpleminded examples, but people do make these kinds of errors. When you see this is about to happen, you should respond by saying, "Let's not introduce that product."

Do my numbers match my strategy?

A common thing that happens within companies is that people make all of these great strategy presentations, management signs off on everything, and then the world shifts completely to a different mode when it's time to put together the profit plan. That is the moment of truth for whether your resource allocation is consistent with what you claim your strategy is, and I'm willing to bet that this is where the biggest disconnect usually takes place.

I therefore looked at plans and expenditure requests from the standpoint of what story the numbers told us about our strategy and whether the two matched or not. When we intended to increase our rate of innovation, one test would be what was happening to the level of R&D spending. When we expected to increase our market share, key tests would be what was happening to spending on promoting our products and the share of capital projects related to new products.

If you've got a 5 percent market share and somebody else in the industry has 40 percent, the idea that you're going to make dramatic gains in market share within a relatively short period of time is just unrealistic.

David Speiser, Science Applications International Corporation (SAIC)

David Speiser is the senior vice president for strategy at SAIC, a scientific, engineering, and technology applications company headquartered in the United States. He also is an alumnus of McKinsey's Los Angeles office, where he was a principal.

Will it create value?

As an industry, we attract a lot of engineers and former government and military professionals. Therefore, the very basic test of whether something drives financial shareholder value or not is very useful because many people are not so financially focused.

Is it material?

One of my biggest tests is to explore whether a proposal is material. Some folks will get excited about doing something in a very small market. The challenge we face, given limited managerial resources, is to educate people about what would be material to the $11 billion corporation we are today, which is very different from the $2 billion corporation we were 15 years ago.

> When it comes to new strategies, a big test is to make sure that the insights and capabilities underlying them are real and not just a result of PowerPoint engineering.

Is it differentiated?

This is probably the hardest test to pass because one of the challenges you have in a corporation that has very broadly applicable skills is that people want to apply them broadly. If you're trying to apply your skills to a broader set of markets, you have to really think critically about what the current competitors are already offering and what you're going to do that's different. That can be tough, especially when you combine it with the materiality test. There may be nothing you can do, in a segment where you have deep interest and knowledge, that will be material over and above what you're doing. But then when you get outside your comfort zone, achieving differentiation is more challenging.

Is it just 'PowerPoint engineering'?

When it comes to new strategies, a big test is to make sure that the insights and capabilities underlying them are real and not just a result of PowerPoint engineering. We get used to assuming that anything people say they can do, they can do. Because they demonstrate this every day in core markets, proof isn't required. But if you're talking about developing a new growth strategy to penetrate a new market, you have to step back and ask tough questions because the proof isn't being delivered every day. Requiring proof that we're connected with the market, that we've actually spoken to potential customers, that we have the insight we claim to have is ultimately one of the most important jobs of the strategist, in my view.

Gail Lumsden, SABMiller
Gail Lumsden is group head of strategy and planning at SABMiller, a leading global brewer.

Where are we in our strategic journey?

It's very easy to get blinkered and complacent, particularly when you're in a successful business: the tendency is to extend the past into the future and assume that your success will continue. The challenge is to watch out for and take signs to the contrary seriously and to use them as a catalyst to further develop your strategy. Winning is a journey, not a destination, and that means understanding where you are in your strategic journey as a business.

For example, we've significantly outperformed our peers over the last ten years in terms of total returns to shareholders (TRS), which demonstrates that we've had a differentiated strategy: we were ahead of our competitors in acquiring undervalued and underperforming local brewers in emerging markets with strong volume growth and in applying a distinctive business model based on operational and

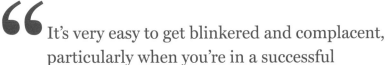

" It's very easy to get blinkered and complacent, particularly when you're in a successful business: the tendency is to extend the past into the future. "

performance-management excellence. In some of those markets, though, per capita consumption growth is now leveling off, and if you look at more recent history, you see that our outperformance in terms of TRS has been abating. So one of the big challenges for us now is how we define and redefine the markets in which we compete.

Are we properly balancing growth and risk?
We're always thinking about opportunities for profitable growth, but we also need to be thinking about the value at risk. Are we protecting our strongholds? Are we adequately thinking about how our competitors will respond to our moves? And in markets where we have a strong leadership position, are we thinking enough about how to create—not just capture—value as the market matures?

Jeffrey Elton, KEW Group
Jeffrey Elton is the CEO and vice chairman of KEW Group, a personalized oncology care network he helped found. Previously, he was senior vice president of strategy and global COO at the Novartis Institutes for BioMedical Research and, before that, a principal in McKinsey's Boston office.

What are the facts?
Pharma and health care delivery are long-cycle businesses where strategy is about optimizing resource reallocation—getting really straight about what investments are going to drive your future earnings. That starts with getting the facts right: there's a lot of hearsay and lore, even though the industry is scientifically driven. It's amazing how much of this is not rooted in fact. So the first set of questions we always spend time on is what's really working or not working, and understanding what "working" actually means.

 Sometimes you have an insight, but that insight is a very small proportion of what's really required to solve a problem. **99**

Is the problem solvable, and do we care?

Sometimes you have an insight, but that insight is a very small proportion of what's really required to solve a problem. You need to determine if, based on what we know now, the problem is solvable. Then, even if it is, do we care? We usually are trying to work on things where we think there's a relatively high unmet medical need. If we work on diseases that impose a high cost burden, this approach helps assure a favorable set of economics, even if we can't predict all the different aspects of reimbursement.

Who can solve that problem?

We presume that we can't possibly have all the talent and capabilities needed to solve any one problem, so what institutions—what companies, specifically—should we be trying to collaborate with to solve this problem confidently and remarkably? Of course, we also need to ask what we need inside this company to successfully engage with that external network. If we don't have people who know a class of problem exceptionally well, we can't even do a good job on due diligence and access the best talent or partners. So this question could help drive our acquisition, talent, or recruitment strategy.

Why might we fail?

Usually, projects or new therapeutics are going to fail for one or two reasons. Running a killer experiment, focused on likely sources of failure, can actually save a lot more time than a pilot that's likely to confirm that this is an interesting area to be in, where we may be able to do something.

How can we shape the market?

In any high-innovation area, there's a heavy dose of "shaping"—both of the market and of the environment you will be walking into—that needs to take place to make this market worth getting into. Getting specific about what you have the ability to shape, and which points of influence you can begin to put in place, is invaluable. o

Boost supply chain resiliency

If you have a global supply chain, you face a troubling new normal: rising complexity and uncertainty are boosting the odds that decisions you make today about manufacturing and supply locations will become uneconomic tomorrow. How can you prepare for the unexpected? Reconfigure monolithic supply chains into nimbler, complexity-busting "splinters," while wielding that network as a hedge against uncertainty. And don't forget the organization: only by tearing down silos and spurring collaboration can you ensure that your company masters the new environment.

Artwork by Josh Cochran

Building the supply chain of the future

Yogesh Malik, Alex Niemeyer, and Brian Ruwadi

Getting there means ditching today's monolithic model in favor of splintered supply chains that dismantle complexity, and using manufacturing networks to hedge uncertainty.

Many global supply chains are not equipped to cope with the world we are entering. Most were engineered, some brilliantly, to manage stable, high-volume production by capitalizing on labor-arbitrage opportunities available in China and other low-cost countries. But in a future when the relative attractiveness of manufacturing locations changes quickly—along with the ability to produce large volumes economically—such standard approaches can leave companies dangerously exposed.

That future, spurred by a rising tide of global uncertainty and business complexity, is coming sooner than many companies expect. Some of the challenges (turbulent trade and capital flows, for example) represent perennial supply chain worries turbocharged by the recent downturn. Yet other shifts, such as those associated with the developing world's rising wealth and the emergence of credible suppliers from these markets, will have supply chain implications for decades to come. The bottom line for would-be architects of manufacturing and supply chain strategies is a greater risk of making key decisions that become uneconomic as a result of forces beyond your control.

Against this backdrop, a few pioneering supply chain organizations are preparing themselves in two ways. First, they are "splintering" their traditional supply chains into smaller, nimbler ones better prepared to manage higher levels of complexity. Second, they are treating their supply chains as hedges against uncertainty by reconfiguring their manufacturing footprints to weather a range of potential outcomes. A look at how the leaders are preparing today offers insights for other companies hoping to get more from their supply chains in the years to come.

Twin challenges

The stakes couldn't be higher. "In our industry," says Jim Owens, the former chairman and CEO of construction-equipment maker Caterpillar, "the competitor that's best at managing the supply chain is probably going be the most successful competitor over time. It's a condition of success."[1] Yet the legacy supply chains of many global companies are ill-prepared for the new environment's growing uncertainty and complexity.

A more uncertain world

Fully 68 percent of global executives responding to a recent McKinsey survey said that supply chain risk will increase in the coming five years.[2] And no wonder: the financial crisis of 2008 dramatically amplified perennial sources of supply chain uncertainty—notably the trajectory of trade and capital flows, as well as currency values—even as the crisis sparked broader worries about the stability of the financial system and the depth and duration of the resulting recession. While many of these sources of uncertainty persist, it's important to recognize that new, long-term shifts in the global economy will continue to pressure supply chains long after more robust growth returns.

The increasing importance of emerging markets tops the list of these uncertainties. Economic growth there will boost global energy consumption in the coming decade by about one-third. Meanwhile, the voracious appetite of China and other developing countries for such resources as iron ore and agricultural commodities is boosting global prices and making it trickier to configure supply chain assets. Worries about the environment are growing, too, along with uncertainty over the scope and direction of environmental regulation.

These long-term trends have knock-on effects that reinforce still other sources of uncertainty. Growth in developing countries contributes to volatility in global currency markets and to protectionist sentiment in the developed world, for example. What's more, different growth rates across various emerging markets mean that rising labor costs can

---

[1] Jim Owens made this remark in an interview conducted by Hans-Werner Kaas on September 20, 2010. For more from that interview, read "My last 100 days," on page 104.
[2] For more, see "The challenges ahead for supply chains: McKinsey Global Survey results," mckinseyquarterly.com, November 2010.

quickly change the relative attractiveness of manufacturing locations. This past summer in China, for example, labor disputes—and a spate of worker suicides—contributed to overnight wage increases of 20 percent or more in some Chinese cities. Bangladesh, Cambodia, and Vietnam experienced similar wage-related strikes and walkouts.[3] Finally, as companies in developing markets increasingly become credible suppliers, deciding which low-cost market to source from becomes more difficult.

Another uncertainty
Protectionism could change the economics of a supply chain at the stroke of a pen. Our research suggests, for example, that the total landed cost of making assembled mechanical products such as washing machines in a given low-cost country could plausibly swing up to 20 percent given different tariff scenarios.

Rising complexity

Manufacturing and supply chain planners must also deal with rising complexity. For many companies, this need means working harder to meet their customers' increasingly diverse requirements. Mobile-phone makers, for example, introduced 900 more varieties of handsets in 2009 than they did in 2000. Proliferation also affects mature product categories: the number of variants in baked goods, beverages, cereal, and confectionery, for instance, all rose more than 25 percent a year between 2004 and 2006, and the number of SKUs[4] at some large North American grocers exceeded 100,000 in 2009.

Meanwhile, globalization brings complexities as rising incomes in developing countries make them extremely desirable as markets, not just manufacturing hubs. Efficient distribution in emerging markets requires creativity, since retail formats typically range from modern hypermarkets to subscale mom-and-pop stores. In Brazil, for example, Nestlé is experimenting with the use of supermarket barges to sell directly to low-income customers along two tributaries of the Amazon River.[5]

Meeting the challenge

In such a world, the idea that companies can optimize their supply chains once—and for all circumstances and customers—is a fantasy. Recognizing this, a few forward-looking companies are preparing in two ways. First, they are splintering their traditional monolithic supply chains into smaller and more flexible ones. While these new supply chains may rely on the same assets and network resources as the old,

---

[3] Tim Johnston, "Striking Cambodian workers reflect Asia trend," *Financial Times*, September 13, 2010.
[4] Stock-keeping units.
[5] Tom Muiler and Iuri Dantas, "Nestlé to sail Amazon Rivers to reach emerging-market consumers," *Bloomberg News*, June 17, 2010.

they use information very differently—helping companies to embrace complexity while better serving customers.

Second, leading companies treat their supply chains as dynamic hedges against uncertainty by actively and regularly examining—even reconfiguring—their broader supply networks with an eye toward economic conditions five or ten years ahead. In doing so, these companies are building diverse and more resilient portfolios of supply chain assets that will be better suited to thrive in a more uncertain world.

From one to many

Splintering monolithic supply chains into smaller, nimbler ones can help tame complexity, save money, and serve customers better. Let's look at an example.

Splintering supply chains: A case study

A US-based consumer durables manufacturer was losing ground to competitors because of problems with its legacy supply chain. Years before, the company—like many global manufacturers—had sent the lion's share of its production to China while maintaining a much smaller presence in North America to stay close to the majority of its customers. One legacy of the move: all of its plants, relying on a unified production-planning process, essentially manufactured the full range of its thousands of products and their many components.

Now, however, increasingly volatile patterns of customer demand, coupled with product proliferation in the form of hundreds of new SKUs each year, were straining the company's supply chain to the point where forecasting- and service-related problems were dissatisfying key customers.

In response, the company examined its portfolio of products and components along two dimensions: the volatility of demand for each SKU it sold and the overall volume of SKUs produced per week. Armed with the resulting matrix, the company began rethinking its supply chain configuration.

Ultimately, the company decided to split its one-size-fits-all supply chain into four distinct splinters. For high-volume products with relatively stable demand (less than 10 percent of SKUs but representing the majority of revenues), the company kept the sourcing and production in China. Meanwhile, the facilities in North America became

Grouping products by demand volatility and overall volume can shed light on how to optimize the supply chain.

Volume and demand volatility by finished-good SKU,[1] example of US-based consumer-durables company

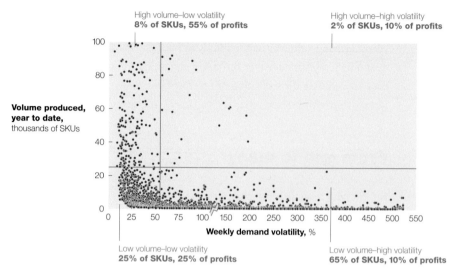

High volume–low volatility
8% of SKUs, 55% of profits

High volume–high volatility
2% of SKUs, 10% of profits

Volume produced, year to date, thousands of SKUs

Weekly demand volatility, %

Low volume–low volatility
25% of SKUs, 25% of profits

Low volume–high volatility
65% of SKUs, 10% of profits

[1] Stock-keeping unit.

responsible for producing the rest of the company's SKUs, including high- and low-volume ones with volatile demand (assigned to the United States) and low-volume, low-demand-volatility SKUs (divided between the United States and Mexico). Ramping up production in a higher-cost country such as the United States made economic sense even for the low-volume products because the company could get them to market much faster, minimize lost sales, and keep inventories down for many low-volume SKUs. Moreover, the products tended to require more specialized manufacturing processes (in which the highly skilled US workforce excelled) and thus gave the company a chance to differentiate itself in a crowded market.

However, the company didn't just reallocate production resources. In tandem, it changed its information and planning processes significantly. For the portfolio's most volatile SKUs (the ones now produced in the United States), the company no longer tried to predict customer demand at all, choosing instead to manufacture directly to customer orders. Meanwhile, managers at these US plants created a radically simplified forecasting process to account for the remaining products—those with low production runs but more stable demand.

For overseas operations, the company continued to have its Chinese plants produce finished goods on the basis of long-run forecasts, as they had done before. The forecasts were now better, though, because planners were no longer trying to account in their models for the "noise" caused by the products with highly volatile demand.

Together, the changes helped the company reduce its sourcing and manufacturing complexity and to lower its cost of goods sold by about 15 percent. Meanwhile, it improved its service levels and shortened lead times to three days, from an average of ten. Quality also improved across the company's full range of products.

How many splinters?

The first question for organizations exploring multiple supply chains is how many are needed. Answering it requires a close look at the way the supply chain assets that a company uses to manufacture and distribute its products matches up against the strategic aspirations it has for those products and their customers.

This requirement seems obvious, but in practice most companies examine only the second half of the equation in a sophisticated way; they can, for example, readily identify which products they see as leaders on cost, service, innovation, or (most likely) some combination of these. Fewer companies seriously examine the operational trade-offs implicit in such choices, let alone make network decisions based on those trade-offs.

Oftentimes, a good place to start is to analyze the volatility of customer demand for a given product line against historical production volumes and to compare the results against the total landed cost for different production locations. This information provides a rough sense of the speed-versus-cost trade-offs and can even suggest locations where supply chain splinters might ultimately be located. A global consumer-packaged-goods maker, for example, quickly saw that two-thirds of the demand associated with a key product line (about 40 percent of the company's product portfolio) could be moved from a higher-cost country to a lower-cost one without hurting customer service.

Of course, companies must carefully check these broad-brush analyses against customer needs. The consumer goods company, for instance, found that packaging innovation was a differentiator for some of its products and thus configured a single production line in the new, lower-cost location to make packaging for several markets quickly. By contrast, in automotive and other assembly-based industries, we find that the customers' responsiveness and the complexity of individual products are important inputs that help determine where supply chains might be splintered.

Second-order benefits

While dividing a supply chain into splinters may seem complicated, in fact this approach allows companies to reduce complexity and manage it better because operational assets can be focused on tasks they're best equipped to handle. At the same time, the added visibility that a splintered approach offers into the guts of a supply chain helps senior managers more effectively employ traditional improvement tools that would have been too overwhelming to tackle before.

After the consumer durables maker divided its supply chain into smaller ones, for example, it was able to use formerly impractical postponement approaches (producing closer in time to demand to keep holding costs low). The company's US plants now combined various SKUs into semifinished components that could quickly be assembled into products to meet customer orders. Indeed, the lower inventory costs this move generated partially offset the higher labor costs of the US factories.

Likewise, the global consumer-packaged-goods maker found that after splintering its supply chain, it was more successful at applying lean-management techniques in its plants. Among the benefits: much faster changeover times in higher-cost production locations, enabling them to handle product-related complexity more effectively.

For more on how to develop scenarios in light of demographic, technological, macroeconomic, and other global trends, see "Applying global trends: A look at China's auto industry," on mckinseyquarterly.com.

Use your network as a hedge

The advantages that multiple supply chains confer are most valuable if companies view them dynamically, with an eye toward the resiliency of the overall supply chain under a variety of circumstances. Will the various strands of a particular global supply network, for example, still make sense if China's currency appreciates by 20 percent, oil costs $90 a barrel, and shipping lanes have 25 percent excess capacity? It's critical for organizations to determine which of the many questions like these are right to ask and to invest energy in understanding the global trends underpinning them. Some companies are already thinking in this way. Nike, for example, long a leader in emerging-market production, manufactured more shoes in Vietnam than in China for the first time in 2010.[6]

[6] Fiscal year.

With better visibility into supply chain operations, companies can achieve bigger efficiency gains.

Example: a consumer durables maker lowers its inventory costs by moving production closer to customer demand

Before

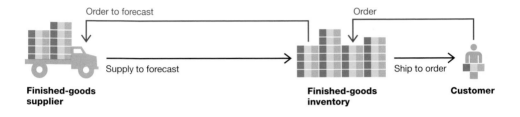

After

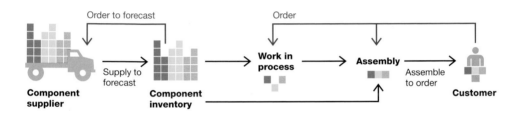

In fact, we believe that the ability of supply chains to withstand a variety of different scenarios could influence the profitability and even the viability of organizations in the not-too-distant future. In light of this, companies should design their portfolios of manufacturing and supplier networks to minimize the total landed-cost risk under different scenarios. The goal should be identifying a resilient manufacturing and sourcing footprint—even when it's not necessarily the lowest-cost one today. This approach calls for a significant mind-set shift not just from operations leaders but also from CEOs and executives across the C-suite.

At the consumer durables manufacturer, for example, senior executives worried that its reliance on China as a hub could become a liability if conditions changed quickly. Consequently, the company's senior team looked at its cost structure and how that might change over the next five to ten years under a range of global wage- and currency-rate conditions. They also considered how the company could be affected by factors such as swinging commodity prices and logistics costs.

While China remained the most attractive manufacturing option in the short term, Mexico was preferable under several plausible scenarios.

The company determined that while China remained the most attractive manufacturing option in the short term, the risks associated with wage inflation and currency-rate changes were real enough to make Mexico a preferable alternative under several plausible scenarios. Consequently, the company has begun quietly building its supplier base there in anticipation of ramping up its manufacturing presence so that it can quickly flex production between China and Mexico should conditions so dictate.

Similarly, the global consumer-packaged-goods manufacturer is examining where dormant capacity in alternative low-cost countries might help it hedge against a range of labor cost, tariff, tax, and exchange-rate scenarios. The company is also factoring in unexpected supply disruptions, including fires, earthquakes, and labor-related strife.

A North American industrial manufacturer chose to broaden its footprint in Brazil and Mexico to hedge against swings in foreign-exchange rates. In particular, the company invested in spare capacity to make several innovative, high-end components that it had formerly produced only in Europe and the United States because of the advanced machining and engineering required. The investment is helping the company hedge against currency swings by quickly transferring production of the components across its global network to match economic conditions. Moreover, the arrangement helps it better support its supply partners as they serve important growth markets.

●   ●   ●

Making these kinds of moves isn't easy, of course, since any alterations to a company's supply chain have far-ranging implications throughout the organization. For starters, such changes require much more cooperation and information sharing across business units than many companies are accustomed to. Indeed, the organizational challenges are so significant that for many companies, a hands-on effort by the CEO and others across the C-suite is needed for success (see the accompanying article, "Is your top team undermining your supply chain?" on the following page).

Nonetheless, the rewards are worthwhile. By creating more resilient and focused supply chains that can thrive amid heightened uncertainty and complexity, companies will gain significant advantages in the coming years. ○

The authors wish to acknowledge Sebastien Katch for his valuable contributions to this article.

Yogesh Malik and **Brian Ruwadi** are principals in McKinsey's Cleveland office; **Alex Niemeyer** is a director in the Miami office.

Is your top team undermining your supply chain?

Christoph Glatzel, Jochen Großpietsch, and Ildefonso Silva

Building bridges between senior managers is a critical step in constructing tomorrow's global supply chain.

Creating a global supply chain that is equipped to thrive in a world of rising complexity and uncertainty involves more than reconfiguring operational assets and making long-term strategic bets about production-and supply-related risks. Significant organizational challenges are involved, too, since the decisions and activities of a company's supply chain group influence (and are influenced by) the sales team, marketers, and product developers, among others.

The result is a host of thorny trade-offs. Should a company, say, move a product to a low-cost manufacturing facility to save money if that means lengthening delivery times? What if trimming the company's product portfolio to reduce manufacturing complexity and costs could stifle marketing efforts to reach new customers? When do the benefits of improved customer service warrant the additional operating expenses required to deliver it?

Supply chain, sales, and marketing managers invariably view such trade-offs through the lens of their own responsibilities—and this perspective often leads to disagreements or misunderstandings. Indeed, a recent McKinsey survey of global executives cited the inability of functional groups to understand their impact on one another as the most common barrier to collaboration for resolving the major supply chain trade-offs.

For more on how executives manage supply chain trade-offs, see "The challenges ahead for supply chains: McKinsey Global Survey results," on mckinseyquarterly.com.

Ineffective collaboration has long been a supply chain sore spot, but its costs are set to rise drastically. If it's hard to agree on the right response to a disruption in a supply chain today, it will be more difficult still when companies deal with multiple interconnected supply chains, each possibly requiring a different solution. And consider the short- and long-term supply chain trade-offs executives must balance in a world where one business unit might be asked to shift its manufacturing lines to a more expensive near-shore location today to build capacity as a hedge against potential future spikes in labor or transport costs.

Finding mechanisms to solve these and other difficult supply chain questions will require hands-on attention from the CEO and other company leaders. The process begins when executives work together to identify places where better information sharing and teamwork will generate the most impact. Let's look, then, at three of the biggest collaboration tensions we routinely observe and see how companies are bridging these organizational divides to create more flexible and capable supply chains.

Tension 1: **Supply chain versus sales**

Supply chain organizations wage a constant battle against volatile demand, and for good reason. An unexpected spike in orders, for example, has expensive consequences in labor and distribution costs. Similarly, inaccurate sales forecasts can lead to stock-outs, lost sales, or excess inventory that must be sold at a discount. Sales and supply chain groups therefore devote significant energy to creating sophisticated planning and forecasting processes in an attempt to predict demand volatility—and blame each other when things go awry.

When these groups work together more closely, they can move beyond the traditional planning-cycle blame game, discover the root causes of volatility, and ultimately begin to influence it. This approach brings tangible business benefits—often quickly. Crucially, over the longer term, the experience that groups gain from flexing their collaborative muscles heightens the ability to react quickly, and in a concerted way, to unforeseen events. That skill will be even more necessary given the increasing uncertainty in the supply chain environment. Here are two examples that illustrate the potential.

The first involves an automotive supplier whose sales teams often scrambled to meet quarterly targets that would guarantee them better performance bonuses. Customers recognized this behavior and, in some cases, were gaming the system by withholding orders until the end of the quarter to secure deeper discounts—creating supply chain headaches *and* hurting the company's bottom line. The vice president of sales and the supply chain head collaborated to fix this problem and make demand more predictable. One key step: substantially trimming end-of-quarter discounts and instead using a price and discount structure based on sales volumes, product loyalty, and participation in promotional efforts. The company also created new incentives to encourage sales teams to spread sales more evenly across the quarter.

Our second example involves a global manufacturer of consumer packaged goods. This company discovered that promotional activity in just five customer accounts drove most of its demand volatility. Although it carefully planned the promotions to maximize revenues, its marketers hadn't thought about the impact on the supply chain. By staggering the promotions over several months and aligning them carefully with baseline demand patterns, the company reduced the overall volatility of demand by 25 percent.

When the company rolled out the new promotions plan, its managers identified another problem: many customers lacked the resources to manage their order levels efficiently and therefore sporadically placed unnecessarily large orders. The company responded by bringing together its sales and supply chain personnel and working with these customers to create better ordering processes for them. In this way, it smoothed the flow of orders—a move that benefitted both parties.

Problems like these are endemic in many supply chains. By tackling these problems, companies often enjoy immediate benefits while building collaborative capabilities that will be crucial over the long term in the more complex and uncertain supply chain environment of the future.

Tension 2: **Supply chain versus service**

A second important tension that has long existed, but will become even more acute as companies seek to create more resilient global supply chains, involves the setting of customer service levels. How speedy should deliveries be? Should some customers receive orders faster than others? What levels of product availability should be guaranteed? In our experience, companies traditionally leave these decisions to the sales function, which often makes service-related decisions without understanding the operational implications or costs involved.

When these groups work together to analyze the full impact of a service decision, they avoid this pitfall—a lesson learned by a chemical company whose sales personnel were pushing its logistics team to reduce delivery times to two days, from three. The company achieved this goal, but only by using more warehouse space and labor and by loading its delivery trucks less efficiently than it otherwise would have. All this increased distribution costs by 5 percent.

While this trade-off might have been acceptable under the right circumstances, a closer examination by the heads of the supply chain and sales groups revealed that most customers didn't mind if deliveries arrived in two, three, or even five days. The real breakpoint when service was most highly valued was 24 hours. By extending the delivery window for normal orders back to three days, the company returned its distribution costs to their original levels. Meanwhile, it launched a special 24-hour express service for critical deliveries, for which it charged a premium. The move ultimately raised the company's costs slightly, but this was more than offset by the new business it generated.

As supply chains splinter and companies diversify production to hedge against uncertainty, the importance of making smart trade-offs about service levels and speed can only grow. Companies seeking to cope will have to strengthen partnerships between the leaders of the supply chain, sales, and service.

Tension 3: **Supply chain versus product proliferation**

Remedying some of the root causes of growing supply chain complexity will be another important benefit of enhanced collaboration in the C-suite. Take the complexity associated with product portfolios. Sales and marketing organizations work hard to create new products, explore new market opportunities, and respond to emerging customer needs. As they do, products and variants tend to proliferate, creating portfolios with long tails of niche offerings. A consumer goods maker we know, for example, recently found that nearly one-third of the 6,400 SKUs[1] in its product portfolio together represented just 1 percent of total revenues.

[1] Stock-keeping units.

This complexity comes at a cost, since low-volume products cost more to make per unit than high-volume ones (because of economies of scale). The consumer goods maker, for example, found that production costs for low-volume products were 129 percent higher than those for its best sellers. Low-volume products also require disproportionate effort in sales and administrative processes. Finally, they drive up supply chain costs: a company must hold higher inventory levels to meet agreed service levels across a broad range of low-volume products than it does over a narrow range of high-volume ones. When all these extra costs are taken into account, the impact can be eye opening. One company we studied found that 25 percent of its SKUs actually *lost* money.

In the face of these numbers, companies might be tempted to take an ax to the long tails of their product portfolios. Yet blind cutting based on sales figures alone often does more harm than good. Some low-volume products have benefits that outweigh their costs, and only through close collaboration across functional boundaries can companies make the right decisions. Such collaboration won't eliminate the need for more carefully segmented supply chain strategies, but it should help ensure that such efforts are well targeted.

Putting it all together

The top of the organization is the right place for most companies to begin negotiating the functional trade-offs we've outlined. But many senior-management teams give precious little attention to supply chain issues. Across the trade-offs our survey explored, for example, no more than 26 percent of the respondents said that their companies reach alignment among functions as part of the supply chain decision-making process. Moreover, 38 percent say that the CEO has no or limited involvement in driving supply chain strategy.

This is a mistake. CEOs set the agenda for their leadership teams, and it is up to CEOs to encourage and facilitate meaningful discussion of important cross-functional supply chain issues. CEOs can go further too. In some of the most impressive supply chains we've seen, the chief executive promotes collaboration and performance improvement with missionary zeal. The CEO of an apparel company, for example, would always make a point, during store visits, of asking shop floor staff how its recent commercial decisions had affected store operations, including logistics. He would bring up this feedback in meetings with purchasing and supply chain teams and continually encouraged his managers to follow up themselves and engage with shop floor staff on similar topics.

CEOs looking to get started can benefit from asking themselves five questions, which in our experience can help leaders begin to ferret out situations where faulty collaboration may be preventing supply chains from reaching their full potential.

1. Is production capacity being developed in the right locations—both for today and the future?

2. Is the sales group doing all it can to make demand smooth and predictable?

3. Are customers offered the service levels they really need?

4. Is my marketing department calling for too many niche products that may be too costly to supply?

5. Are our purchasing and sourcing decisions being made with their supply chain implications in mind?

● ● ●

Poor collaboration and silo thinking have long thwarted the efforts of companies to get more from their supply chains. In a future characterized by rising complexity and uncertainty, solving this perennial problem will change from a valuable performance enhancer to a competitive necessity. ○

Christoph Glatzel is a principal in McKinsey's Cologne office, **Jochen Großpietsch** is a principal in the Barcelona office, and **Ildefonso Silva** is a principal in the São Paulo office.

Stop the madness of knowledge work

If you are like most senior executives, you cope with nonstop meetings and a constant barrage of e-mail through multitasking. It's time to desist: task juggling undermines creativity and distracts you from your real job of digging in on difficult, important decisions. Read about the techniques some senior leaders are using to focus and to reset impossible demands. And learn from Tom Davenport how you can boost the productivity of knowledge workers by tailoring technology to individual roles. By structuring the information morass, you can ease your organization's pain.

Artwork by Scott Bakal

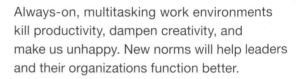

Recovering from information overload

Derek Dean and Caroline Webb

Always-on, multitasking work environments kill productivity, dampen creativity, and make us unhappy. New norms will help leaders and their organizations function better.

For all the benefits of the information technology and communications revolution, it has a well-known dark side: information overload and its close cousin, attention fragmentation. These scourges hit CEOs and their colleagues in the C-suite particularly hard because senior executives so badly need uninterrupted time to synthesize information from many different sources, reflect on its implications for the organization, apply judgment, make trade-offs, and arrive at good decisions.

The importance of reserving chunks of time for reflection, and the difficulty of doing so, have been themes in management writing for decades. Look no further than Peter Drucker's 1967 classic, *The Effective Executive*,[1] which emphasized that "most of the tasks of the executive require, for minimum effectiveness, a fairly large quantum of time." Drucker's solutions for fragmented executives—reserve large blocks of time on your calendar, don't answer the phone, and return calls in short bursts once or twice a day—sound remarkably like the ones offered up by today's time- and information-management experts.[2]

---

[1] Peter Drucker, *The Effective Executive*, Oxford, UK: Butterworth-Heinemann, 1967, pp. 28–29.

[2] For example, compare Julie Morgenstern's advice to "control the time nibblers," in her well-regarded book, *Never Check E-mail in the Morning: And Other Unexpected Strategies for Making your Work Life Work* (Fireside, 2005), with Drucker's statement that "to be effective, every knowledge worker, and especially every executive, needs to be able to dispose of time in fairly large chunks."

Yet they are devilishly difficult to implement, and getting more so all the time. Every challenge recounted by Drucker in 1967 remains today: an unceasing rhythm of daily meetings, a relentless expectation of travel to connect with customers and far-flung reaches of the organization, an inordinate number of opportunities to represent the company at dinners and events. Add to these challenges a torrent of e-mail, huge volumes of other information, and an expanding variety of means—from the ever-present telephone to blogs, tweets, and social networks—through which executives can connect with their organizations and customers, and you have a recipe for exhaustion. Many senior executives literally have two overlapping workdays: the one that is formally programmed in their diaries and the one "before, after, and in-between," when they disjointedly attempt to grab spare moments with their laptops or smart phones, multitasking in a vain effort to keep pace with the information flowing toward them.

Better solutions exist, and they aren't rocket science.[3] What we hope to do in this article is help executives, and their organizations, by reminding them of three simple things. First, multitasking is a terrible coping mechanism. A body of scientific evidence demonstrates fairly conclusively that multitasking makes human beings less productive, less creative, and less able to make good decisions. If we want to be effective leaders, we need to stop.

Second, addressing information overload requires enormous self-discipline. A little like recovering addicts, senior executives must labor each day to keep themselves on track by applying timeless yet powerful guidelines: find time to focus, filter out the unimportant, forget about work every now and then. The holy grail, of course, is to retain the benefits of connectivity without letting it distract us too much.

Third, since senior executives' behavior sets the tone for the organization, they have a duty to set a better example. The widespread availability of powerful communications technologies means employees now share many of the time- and attention-management challenges of their leaders. The whole organization's productivity can now be affected by information overload, and no single person or group can address it in isolation. Resetting the culture to healthier norms is a critical new responsibility for 21st-century executives.

[3] For another view on today's information challenge and some potential solutions, see Paul Hemp, "Death by information overload," *Harvard Business Review*, September 2009, Volume 87, Number 9, pp. 82–89.

The perils of multitasking

We tend to believe that by doing several things at the same time we can better handle the information rushing toward us and get more done. What's more, multitasking—interrupting one task with another—can sometimes be fun. Each vibration of our favorite high-tech e-mail device carries the promise of potential rewards. Checking it may provide a welcome distraction from more difficult and challenging tasks. It helps us feel, at least briefly, that we've accomplished something— even if only pruning our e-mail in-boxes. Unfortunately, current research indicates the opposite: multitasking unequivocally damages productivity.

It slows us down

The root of the problem is that our brain is best designed to focus on one task at a time. When we switch between tasks, especially complex ones, we become startlingly less efficient: in a recent study, for example, participants who completed tasks in parallel took up to 30 percent longer and made twice as many errors as those who completed the same tasks in sequence. The delay comes from the fact that our brains can't successfully tell us to perform two actions concurrently.[4] When we switch tasks, our brains must choose to do so, turn off the cognitive rules for the old task, and turn on the rules for the new one. This takes time, which reduces productivity, particularly for heavy multitaskers— who, it seems, take even longer to switch between tasks than occasional multitaskers.[5]

In practice, most of us would probably acknowledge that multitasking lets us quickly cross some of the simpler items off our to-do lists. But it rarely helps us solve the toughest problems we're working on. More often than not, it's procrastination in disguise.

It hampers creativity

One might think that constant exposure to new information at least makes us more creative. Here again, the opposite seems to be true. Teresa Amabile and her colleagues at the Harvard Business School evaluated the daily work patterns of more than 9,000 individuals working on projects that required creativity and innovation. They

---

[4] Christopher L. Asplund, Paul E. Dux, Jason Ivanoff, and René Marois, "Isolation of a central bottleneck of information processing with time-resolved fMRI," *Neuron*, 2006, Volume 52, Number 6, pp. 1109–20.

[5] Eyal Ophir, Clifford Nass, and Anthony D. Wagner, "Cognitive control in media multitaskers," *PNAS*, 2009, Volume 106, Number 37, pp. 15583–87.

We are at risk of moving toward an ever less thoughtful and creative professional reality unless we stop now to redesign our working norms.

found that the likelihood of creative thinking is higher when people focus on one activity for a significant part of the day and collaborate with just one other person. Conversely, when people have highly fragmented days—with many activities, meetings, and discussions in groups—their creative thinking decreases significantly.[6]

These findings also make intuitive sense. Creative problem solving typically requires us to hold several thoughts at once "in memory," so we can sense connections we hadn't seen previously and forge new ideas. When we bounce around quickly from thought to thought, we know we're less likely to make those crucial connections.

It makes us anxious and it's addictive

In laboratory settings, researchers have found that subjects asked to multitask show higher levels of stress hormones.[7] A survey of managers conducted by Reuters revealed that two-thirds of respondents believed that information overload had lessened job satisfaction and damaged their personal relationships. One-third even thought it had damaged their health.[8]

Nonetheless, evidence is emerging that humans can become quite addicted to multitasking. Edward Hallowell and John Ratey from Harvard, for instance, have written about people for whom feeling connected provides something like a "dopamine squirt"—the neural effects follow the same pathways used by addictive drugs.[9] This effect is familiar too: who hasn't struggled against the urge to check the smart phone when it vibrates, even when we're in the middle of doing something else?

[6] Teresa M. Amabile et al., "Time pressure and creativity in organizations: A longitudinal field study," Harvard Business School working paper, Number 02-073, 2002.

[7] Sue Shellenbarger, "Multitasking makes you stupid," *Wall Street Journal*, February 27, 2003.

[8] David Bawden and Lyn Robinson, "The dark side of information: Overload, anxiety, and other paradoxes and pathologies," *Journal of Information Science*, Volume 20, Number 10, pp. 1–12.

[9] Edward M. Hallowell, MD, and John J. Ratey, MD, *Delivered from Distraction*, Ballantine Books, 2006.

Coping with the deluge

So if multitasking isn't the answer, what is? In our conversations with CEOs and other executives trying to cope, we heard repeatedly about some fairly basic strategies that aren't very different in spirit from the ones Drucker described more than 40 years ago: some combination of focusing, filtering, and forgetting. The challenge for these executives, and all of us, is that executing such strategies in an always-on environment is harder than it was when Drucker was writing. It requires a tremendous amount of self-discipline, and we can't do it alone: in our teams and across the whole organization, we need to establish a set of norms that support a more productive way of working.

Focus

The calendars of CEOs and other senior executives are often booked back-to-back all day, sometimes in 15-minute increments. Gary Loveman, CEO of Harrah's Entertainment, describes the implication: "You have to guard against the danger of overeating at an interesting intellectual buffet. I often need to cover a lot of functional terrain over the course of a day, but I'm careful not to be too light on deserving topics and to make the time to get to meaningful depth on the most important ones."[10] Digital information overload compounds the peril of "overeating" by flooding leaders with a variety of questions and topics that frequently could be addressed by others, thereby distracting those leaders from the thorny, unpleasant, and high-stakes problems where they are most needed.

Many executives respond through the old strategy of creating "alone time." Applied Materials CEO Mike Splinter, for example, finds time between 6:30 and 8:00 AM; Dame Christine Beasley, England's chief nursing officer, uses her traveling time; Brent Assink, executive director of the San Francisco Symphony, schedules any time he can find in the middle of the day. Bill Gross, chief investment officer at Pacific Investment Management Company (PIMCO), takes an extreme approach: "I don't answer or look at any e-mails I don't want to. I don't have a cell phone; I don't have a BlackBerry. My motto is, 'I don't want to be connected; I want to be disconnected.'"[11]

None of this can work, says Assink, unless the management team knows it must keep moving throughout the day without rapid-fire input from the top. Assink has been explicit with his staff: "If they want an

---

[10]All unattributed quotes are taken from interviews conducted by the authors.
[11]Alex Taylor III et al., "How I work," *Fortune*, March 15, 2006.

immediate response, it will have to be a phone call. If they send an e-mail they will get a response at the end of the day."

What about the relentless barrage of information that pours in? Managing it may be as simple—and difficult—as switching off the input. Shut down e-mail, close Web browsers, have phone calls go automatically to voice mail, and let your assistant and team know that you are in a focused working session. Christine Beasley says, "If you're really addicted and can't be trusted not to check the BlackBerry when it's in your pocket or bag, you just have to leave it behind."

Filter

Of course, turning everything off just means that your inbox will be overflowing when you reconnect. And there's a danger of throwing out the baby with the bathwater: no one wants to lose the ability to stay in touch easily with the organization, customers, and other stakeholders or to "give a short and direct answer to quick questions," as Mike Splinter puts it, adding that "you don't want to be the blockade in the business cycle."

A good filtering strategy, therefore, is critical. It starts with giving up the fiction that leaders need to be on top of everything, which has taken hold as information of all types has become more readily and continuously accessible. Rather, plain old delegation is as important with information as it always has been with tasks. As Gary Loveman says, "Keeping current on what is going on takes a lot of my time, but I only engage in depth personally on those issues that are best served by my involvement and are critical to the company's performance, either now or in the future." Christine Beasley has a similar view: "You cannot read everything. The things that I do look at are the things that matter, the things I really need to make a decision on."

Some leaders now explicitly refuse to respond to any e-mail on which they are only cc'd, to filter out issues that others think require no action from them. You also may need to educate the people around you about what deserves to fill your limited time. Gary Loveman explains that "there is a substantial ante to get my time—you need to do some work, provide me with data and insight, let me read something in advance. That simple bar keeps a lot of the items of lesser importance off my calendar."

Winning respect for your in-box, though, won't get you all the way there. Establishing an effective, day-to-day information-management

support structure has become a critical success factor for senior executives. This structure may be elaborate, including a chief of staff for
the CEO of a major organization, or as simple as a capable assistant
who "is fantastic at managing some of my e-mail traffic, weeding
out the things that I don't really need to see," as Christine Beasley says.

Forget

It bears repeating that giving our brains downtime to process new
intellectual input is a critical element of learning and thinking creatively—
not just according to researchers, but also to corporate leaders. Bill
Gross says, "Some of my best ideas literally come from standing on my
head doing yoga. After about 15 minutes of yoga, all of a sudden some
significant light bulbs seem to turn on."[12] Mike Splinter also sees value
in physical exercise: "I find that just staying in shape helps me be
more mentally crisp every day."

Getting outside helps—recent research has found that people learn
significantly better after a walk in nature compared with a walk in
the city.[13] And emotional interaction with other people can also divert
attention from conscious intellectual processing, a good step toward
engaging the unconscious. Sheri McCoy, chairman of Johnson & Johnson
Pharmaceuticals Group, explains, "When I go home at night, I like
to just say, 'OK, I'm not looking at my BlackBerry for two or three hours.'
I'm just relaxing. I feel like that lets me conserve my energy and
focus later." Christine Beasley has rules that protect her personal time
at weekends, reasoning that "people can always get hold of me if
it's urgent."

[12] Alex Taylor III et al., "How I work," *Fortune*, March 15, 2006.
[13] Matt Richtel, "Digital devices deprive brain of needed downtime," *New York Times*,
August 24, 2010.

A responsibility to hit the 'reset button'

All this was easier back in Drucker's day, when we couldn't talk on the phone during the daily commute, we didn't bring multiple connectivity-enabling devices with us on vacation, and planes didn't have Wi-Fi. The strategies of focusing, filtering, and forgetting are also tougher to implement now because of the norms that have developed around 21st-century teamwork. Most leaders today would feel guilty if they didn't respond to an e-mail within 24 hours. Few feel comfortable "hiding" from their teams during the day (or on the drive home or during the evening) in order to focus more intently on the most complex issues. And there is the personal satisfaction that comes from feeling needed.

But there is a business responsibility to reset these norms, given how markedly information overload decreases the quality of learning and decision making. Multitasking is not heroic; it's counterproductive. As the technological capacity for the transmission and storage of information continues to expand and quicken, the cognitive pressures on us will only increase. We are at risk of moving toward an ever less thoughtful and creative professional reality unless we stop now to redesign our working norms.

First, we need to acknowledge and reevaluate the mind-sets that attach us to our current patterns of behavior. We have to admit, for example, that we do feel satisfied when we can respond quickly to requests and that doing so somewhat validates our desire to feel so necessary to the business that we rarely switch off. There's nothing wrong with these feelings, but we need to consider them alongside their measurable cost to our long-term effectiveness. No one would argue that burning up all of a company's resources is a good strategy for long-term success, and that is equally true of its leaders and their mental resources.

Second, leaders need to become more ruthless than ever about stepping back from all but the areas that they alone must address. There's some effort involved in choosing which areas to delegate; it takes skill in coaching others to handle tasks effectively and clarity of expectations on both sides. But with those things in place, a more mindful division of labor creates more time for leaders' focused reflections on the most critical issues and also develops a stronger bench of talent.

Finally, to truly make this approach work, leaders have to redesign working norms together with their teams. One person, even a CEO, cannot do that alone—who wants to be the sole person on the senior team who leaves the smart phone behind when he or she goes on vacation? Absent some explicit discussion, that kind of action could be taken as a lack of commitment to the business, not as a productive attempt to disconnect and recharge. So we encourage leaders and their teams to discuss openly how they choose to focus, filter, and forget; how they support each other in creating the necessary time and space to perform at their best; and how they enable others, throughout the organization, to do the same. This conversation can also be the right starting point for a deeper look at the information and technology needs of all the company's knowledge workers. (For more on how to tackle this thorny problem, see the accompanying article, "Rethinking knowledge work: A strategic approach," on the following page.)

The benefits of lightening the burden of information overload—in productivity, creativity, morale, and business results—will more than justify the effort. And the more we appreciate the benefits, the easier it will be to make new habits stick. o

The authors would like to acknowledge the important contributions that Matthias Birk, a consultant in the Berlin office, made to this article through his research on cognitive sciences.

Derek Dean is an alumnus of McKinsey's San Francisco office, where he was a director; **Caroline Webb** is a principal in the London office.

Rethinking knowledge work: A strategic approach

Thomas H. Davenport

The information needs of knowledge workers vary, depending on the job. The key to improving their productivity is applying technology in a more precise way.

In the half-century since Peter Drucker coined the term "knowledge workers," their share of the workforce has steadily grown—and so has the range of technology tools aimed at boosting their productivity. Yet there's little evidence that massive spending on personal computing, productivity software, knowledge-management systems, and much else has moved the needle. What's more, a wide variety of recent research has begun suggesting that always-on, multitasking work environments are so distracting that they are sapping productivity. (For more on this problem, see "Recovering from information overload," on page 80.)

After researching the productivity of knowledge workers for years, I've concluded that organizations need a radically different approach. Yes, technology is a vital enabler of communication, of collaboration, and of access to rising volumes of information. But least-common-denominator approaches involving more technology for all have reached a point of diminishing returns. It's time for companies to develop a strategy for knowledge work—one that not only provides a clearer view of the types of information that workers need to do their jobs but also recognizes that the application of technology across the organization must vary considerably, according to the tasks different knowledge workers perform.

Few executives realize that there are two divergent paths for improving access to the information that lies at the core of knowledge work.

The most common approach, giving knowledge workers free access to a wide variety of tools and information resources, presumes that these employees will determine their own work processes and needs. The other, the structured provision of information and knowledge, involves delivering them to employees within a well-defined context of tasks and deliverables. Computers send batches of work to employees and provide the information needed to do it.

Both the free-access and structured-provisioning approaches are in wide use, but they make radically different assumptions about how knowledge work should be performed and its productivity improved. Executives who aren't conscious of the trade-offs they are making between them and thus don't look for opportunities to harness the power of structure probably won't get the most from knowledge workers.

Equally important, leaders must pursue IT and productivity opportunities at the right level of granularity. While it might be tempting to think that a given approach will work well for an entire organization, reality is rarely so tidy. In my experience, the unit of analysis should be particular jobs and roles—or at least distinct categories of jobs and roles. To move the needle in a specific business unit or function, it's not enough to launch a set of company-wide initiatives or to count on a piece of software. Instead, leaders of knowledge workers should understand the key differences among them and tailor solutions to these peculiarities.

The free-access approach

Over the past two decades, giving knowledge workers free access to information and knowledge has been the primary way of arming them to do their jobs. The rise of the Internet, the establishment of organizational knowledge-management systems, and, most recently, the advent of social media provide knowledge workers with a vast array of information from public and private sources. More analytically focused knowledge workers may also draw upon warehouses of structured data and quantitative-analysis tools.

In this model, knowledge workers define and integrate their own information environments. The free-access approach has been particularly common among autonomous knowledge workers with high expertise: attorneys, investment bankers, marketers, product designers, professors, scientists, and senior executives, for example. Their work activities are seen as too variable or even idiosyncratic to be modeled or structured with a defined process. Their need for access to IT sources—ranging from the Internet to various online databases and social media to work tools such as e-mail, spreadsheets, presentation tools, and more complex business intelligence analytics—is presumed to be equally eclectic and unpredictable. With an increasingly porous technology barrier between personal lives and jobs, these employees can often be found doing paid work from home and tending to their personal affairs in the office.

In the free-access model, the presumption is that knowledge workers, as experts, know what information is available and can search for and manage it themselves. It's also assumed that they have the discipline to avoid wasting time surfing the Web or watching pornography, sports, or funny YouTube videos at work. Of course, these assumptions may sometimes be incorrect.

In the free-access model, the presumption is that knowledge workers have the discipline to avoid wasting time surfing the Web or watching pornography, sports, or funny YouTube videos. Of course, these assumptions may sometimes be incorrect.

Benefits of the free-access approach

Knowledge workers typically enjoy the free-access approach, which provides plenty of autonomy in their work processes and in how they use information. For employers, this positive feeling is probably useful for retention and job engagement.

Free access is well suited to work where it's difficult to predict contingencies in advance. A structured-process technology would be inadequate, for example, when an investment-banking client suggests a completely novel way of structuring a transaction or, in legal settings, when a key witness becomes unavailable unexpectedly. Free-access approaches allow for creative responses to uncertainty and ambiguity.

The information technology behind the free-access model is relatively easy to implement. The Internet and social media are readily accessible to anyone, and access to third-party databases is possible with any Web browser—although closed company cultures sometimes impede knowledge sharing. Most knowledge workers know how to use basic office productivity tools, and some are even quite skilled at them. Systems integration issues are minor, since workers lie at the center of the information flow.

Shortcomings of the free-access approach

The problems of free access are fairly obvious: while workers may know how to use technology tools, they may not be skilled at searching for, using, or sharing the knowledge. One survey revealed that over a quarter of a typical knowledge worker's time is spent searching for information.[1] Another found that only 16 percent of the content within typical businesses is posted to locations where other workers can access it.[2] Most knowledge workers haven't been trained in search or knowledge management and have an incomplete understanding of how to use data sources and analytical tools.

Productivity losses can be substantial. Even before the advent of social media, workers in one 2005 survey sponsored by America Online and Salary.com cited personal Internet use as the biggest distraction at work. Another study of workplace productivity found that average knowledge workers access their e-mail more than 50 times, use instant messaging 77 times, and visit more than 40 Web sites a day.[3] A UK study suggests that social-media use by knowledge workers costs British companies £6.5 billion a year in lost productivity.[4]

Productivity metrics are nearly nonexistent. If productivity is measured at all, it's only at the highest level, such as legal briefs developed per month, research articles written and published per year, or new drug compounds discovered per decade. Fine-grained monitoring of productivity and information would, of course, help to improve productivity but risks clashing with the spirit of free information access.

[1] Jeff Dance, "Enterprise technology delivers more efficiency (4 of 10)," freshconsulting.com, December 9, 2009.
[2] "Managers say the majority of information obtained for their use is worthless, Accenture survey finds," accenture.com, January 4, 2007.
[3] Tony Wright, "Information overload: Show me the data," blog.rescuetime.com, June 14, 2008.
[4] "Facebook costs UK billions," *GSS Monthly Newsletter*, www.gss.co.uk, February 2008.

The structured provision of knowledge

Structured-provision technologies first appeared in the early 1990s and have improved considerably of late. They often have a range of functions. The most important is workflow technology that controls how knowledge workers get information and job tasks. These workers may encounter supporting technologies that include information portals, business rules or algorithms to automate decisions, document- or content-management systems, business process management-and-monitoring systems, and collaboration tools. Increasingly modular component designs make these technologies easier to deploy.

In corporate parlance, such technologies are often called case-management systems because they allow workers to complete an entire case or unit of work. Such applications include the processing of legal cases, insurance claims, or bank loans; the issuing of permits or licenses; and the completion of interactions with patients in health care. Case management can create value whenever some degree of structure or process can be imposed upon information-intensive work. Until recently, structured-provision approaches have been applied mostly to lower-level information tasks that are repetitive, predictable, and thus easier to automate.

Benefits of the structured model
Productivity is the major benefit: as measured by the completion of key tasks per unit of work time, it often rises by 50 percent when organizations implement these technologies. One automobile-leasing company, for example, achieved such gains after it implemented a new system for lease processing and end-of-lease sale offers. The reason for the improvement was that workers had few distractions and spent no time searching for information.

Adding to the efficiencies, in most cases companies can route tasks globally to any worker with the time and expertise to undertake them; if Sally is away on vacation, the system knows and sends cases to Joe for approval instead. Work processes become more transparent, and it becomes easier to manage them, to exercise approval authority, and to monitor improvements. The structured model also facilitates collaboration and the coordination of tasks. Many implementations help companies engage multiple workers and groups to process cases. These systems also often incorporate business rules or algorithms, determined by an organization's best experts, that help companies decide, say, whether to issue policies, make loans, or pay claims. For managers, these systems can therefore improve the quality and consistency of decision making, while also speeding it up through automation or semi-automation.

Shortcomings of the structured model

The downside of these technologies is negative reactions by the workers who use them. Some managers I have interviewed say that workers feel there is too much structure and too little autonomy in their work; they sometimes feel "chained to their desks." Socialization at work—informal chats in the hallway—can decrease dramatically. In some cases where workers previously had a high degree of autonomy (physicians at an academic medical center, for example), they revolted against such systems. Some organizations that encountered initial resistance found that it decreased over time. Other organizations overcame workers' objections by instituting new forms of social interaction that meshed with improved work processes.

In structured information environments, computer systems rather than knowledge workers integrate the work, so extensive system and process design is required up front for implementation. While these systems can be tailored to fit complex business processes, that kind of tight fit can become a problem if business environments or processes change. When the system includes an automated decision-making component, it's important to monitor the business environment and the outcome of decisions to ensure that the system continues to produce the desired process output. One chilling example of how things can go awry: automated but insufficiently monitored mortgage decisions were among the contributors to the recent financial crisis.

How companies apply these principles

The greatest potential for productivity improvements involves bringing more structured knowledge to workplaces and processes where the free approach has dominated. So far, lower-level process work has been the primary beneficiary of structured-provision tools. However, advancing technologies are making them better suited to tasks that until now have been the preserve of free-access approaches—tasks centered on expert thinking and collaboration. In one example, a major academic medical center is employing "smart forms" that present physicians with all the available information about a particular patient's disease on one screen and even produce first drafts of notes about their interactions with patients for medical records.

Some forward-looking companies are testing more structured approaches in a broader range of work, often with positive results. Here are three areas of progress.

High-level work

Companies have considerable opportunity for applying structured technology and processes to the more routine aspects of even highly collaborative jobs. An insurance company, for example, implemented workflow- and document-management technologies to help develop and modify its investment portfolio. The system replaced numerous spreadsheets and e-mails with a common global system that synchronized communications and transactions among several different groups across several countries. Each group (including operations, funding, controls, and legal) now adds its components to the portfolio. When a new portfolio or modification is completed, the documents are finalized and sent to an external custodian for management and recording. Fund managers find the system relatively noninvasive; if their involvement is needed for a decision or approval, they are notified automatically via e-mail.

Better processes

Technologies are also being used to structure previously unstructured processes. For example, GE Energy Financial Services, which specializes in lending for large energy projects, has worked to boost the productivity and quality of decisions in its loan underwriting. A managing director with responsibilities for the unit's marketing and investment strategy brought together GE analysts and researchers, who extracted typical decision rules from experienced company executives. The rules were embedded in a semi-automated decision system that scores prospective deals and recommends that they be approved or disapproved. Junior analysts can use the system to determine whether a deal is likely to succeed—without taking it to a credit committee comprising senior business unit executives, who can of course override the recommendation if they wish to do so. Deals made using the new approach have generated returns 40 percent higher than the old, unstructured one did.

Hybrid approaches

Some organizations combine the free and structured approaches. One of the easiest ways of doing so is to place partial restrictions on the types of information highly autonomous workers can use—for example, by limiting access to pornography, sports, or social-networking sites while at work. A more nuanced approach allows employees to be both free and structured. Partners Healthcare, which comprises several teaching hospitals in Boston, has a structured system that automatically recommends appropriate drugs and treatments to physicians but allows them to override it. The organization also makes a variety of free-access knowledge databases available to doctors, but the structured system, which incorporates medical knowledge into the process for ordering care, is used much more frequently.

A related approach imposes structured techniques for only some aspects of a job. Some companies, for example, use product-lifecycle-management systems to structure the back end of the product design process but don't use them during the early product conceptualization and brainstorming stages. The key issue here is to decide which aspects of the relevant process could benefit from more structured technologies and processes and which should be left largely untouched by them.

Crafting a strategy for knowledge work

Few organizations have thought systematically about where additional structure could enhance productivity. A good starting point is identifying your knowledge workers and understanding the range of tasks they perform. The unit of analysis should be a particular knowledge job, not the organization as a whole. That's important because different types of knowledge workers within the same organization often have very different knowledge and information requirements. Furthermore, knowledge is more readily structured for some jobs than for others, and some workers can resist imposed structures more than others.

Matching technology and work

I have found the matrix in the exhibit very useful when planning technology strategies for knowledge workers. It is based on my experience that knowledge work generally falls into one of four clusters, each with its own characteristics. These four knowledge work classifications are shaped by two factors: the work's degree of complexity (x-axis) and the level of interdependence among workers who carry out a task (y-axis). Leaders can use this taxonomy as a guide to determine whether a structured, free, or hybrid approach best fits a given job.

The *transaction* cell of the matrix describes knowledge work requiring relatively low amounts of collaboration and judgment, such as employment in call centers, claims processing, and other administrative-intensive roles. Structured-provision approaches fit this type of work well—indeed, it is the only type where they are commonly applied.

Different types of knowledge workers require different kinds of support technologies.

Structured-provision tools are commonly used	Free-access tools are commonly used but structured provision may be applied in some areas	Free-access tools are typically the only successful approach

Collaborative groups	**Integration model** • Systematic, repeatable work • Highly reliant on formal processes, methodologies, or standards • Dependent on tight integration across functional boundaries	**Collaboration model** • Improvisational work • Highly reliant on deep expertise across multiple functions • Dependent on fluid deployment of flexible teams
Individual actors	**Transaction model** • Routine work • Highly reliant on formal rules, procedures, and training • Dependent on low-discretion workforce or on automation	**Expert model** • Judgment-oriented work • Highly reliant on individual expertise and experience • Dependent on star performers

Level of interdependence

Routine   Interpretation/judgment

Complexity of work

One example is a call center system that channels calls from customers to workers, along with all the information and knowledge needed to meet the customers' needs. Another would be an insurance-claims-processing system that delivers all necessary documents and forms to claims workers.

As the degree of collaboration required for a job moves up into the exhibit's *integration* cell, free-access tools become widely available. It is common to find work circulating by way of e-mail and voluntary collaboration and much less common to find structured-provision technologies. Yet there are some semistructured exceptions, including lower-level roles in software development, engineering, and product design and development. The aforementioned product-lifecycle-management system that tracks designs, components, and approvals might help structure the work of certain engineers, for example.

In the exhibit's *expert* cell, the goal is to apply expert knowledge to tasks or problems. The relevant knowledge traditionally is stored in the expert's brain, but today many organizations want to supplement it with online knowledge. Although free-access technologies are typically the chief means of accessing it, in some instances structured approaches can be applied, particularly when productivity and online-knowledge access are equally important. In such cases, the organization must find some way for a computer to mediate the expert's job, so that knowledge can be embedded in the flow of the work process, as some health care organizations have done with intelligent order entry systems for providers. Similarly, a few leading IT-consulting firms are attempting to bring more structure to the delivery of various IT services by using online tools. Expert jobs may also benefit from "guided" data-mining and decision analysis applications for work involving quantitative data: software leads the expert through the analysis and interpretation of data.

Finally, work in the exhibit's *collaboration* cell—which involves knowledge activities such as those of investment bankers crafting big deals, financial analysts creating corporate plans and budgets, marketers developing major marketing plans, attorneys working in teams on large cases, and scientists playing a part in large scientific projects—is usually iterative and unstructured. Typically, the only tools that succeed in such environments provide free access to information and are used voluntarily by the worker. Although systems involving structured workflows and embedded knowledge aren't entirely beyond the scope of this kind of work, they will be hard to develop. Exceptions might include areas such as knowledge reuse: a group of collaborating attorneys, for example, could recycle a legal brief.

Mastering common challenges

While the classification of work and roles will vary considerably across organizations, the pursuit of productivity through structure typically brings with it at least two common challenges. These are preventing the alienation of formerly free knowledge workers and avoiding automated crack-ups like the ones some financial-services firms experienced with mortgage approvals.

Allowing knowledge workers to override automated or semi-automated decisions can help alleviate both of these problems. Such measures can not only lead to better decisions but also reduce resentment or even rebellion against the system. Of course, if experts constantly override it, you must find out why.

Another way of smoothing the path to structure is letting knowledge workers use familiar, typically free-access tools when they interact with a structured system. To alert them when it's time to use a structured application, for example, have it send them an e-mail. If a structured task requires, say, passing financial information to and from the system, let workers use a spreadsheet. Always remember: high-end knowledge workers don't want to spend all their working hours interacting with automated tools.

Finally, it's critical to ensure that at least some knowledge workers and executives understand how the structured system works, so they can be alert for signs that it is out of kilter with changes in the economic environment or business model. Identifying such mismatches will help organizations know when they should pull the plug on structured systems and return to human judgment—a return that can save them from losing lots of money, fast.

● ● ●

We live in a world where knowledge-based work is expanding rapidly. So is the application of technology to almost every business process and job. But to date, high-end knowledge workers have largely remained free to use only the technology they personally find useful. It's time to think about how to make them more productive by imposing a bit more structure. This combination of technology and structure, along with a bit of managerial discretion in applying them to knowledge work, may well produce a revolution in the jobs that cost and matter the most to contemporary organizations. o

Tom Davenport, an alumnus of McKinsey's New York office, holds the president's chair in information technology and management at Babson College.

Picture This

Urban economic clout moves east

Richard Dobbs, Jaana Remes, and Sven Smit

World's top 50 cities, ranked by GDP[1]

○ Dropout—included in 2007 but not in 2025

● Top 50 city in both 2007 and 2025

● Newcomer—absent in 2007 but included in 2025

[1] GDP is measured in dollars, using market exchange rates in 2007 and predicted real exchange rates in 2025. Data points on map and in lists refer to metropolitan areas rather than specific city jurisdictions, aggregating neighboring cities when appropriate (eg, Rhein-Ruhr in Germany; Los Angeles, Long Beach, and Santa Ana in California; or Mumbai and Thane in India).

Source: McKinsey Global Institute

Richard Dobbs is a director of the McKinsey Global Institute (MGI) and a director in McKinsey's Seoul office; **Jaana Remes** is a senior fellow at MGI; **Sven Smit** is a director in the Amsterdam office.

A forthcoming McKinsey Global Institute report provides more detail on urban economic change, drawing on MGI's database of more than 1,000 cities. The report will be available in February 2011 on mckinsey.com/mgi.

101

More than 20 of the world's top 50 cities ranked by GDP will be located in Asia by the year 2025, up from 8 in 2007. During that same time period, our research suggests, more than half of Europe's top 50 cities will drop off the list, as will 3 in North America. In this new landscape of urban economic power, Shanghai and Beijing will outrank Los Angeles and London, while Mumbai and Doha will surpass Munich and Denver. The implications—for companies' growth priorities, countries' economic relationships, and the world's sustainability strategy—are profound.

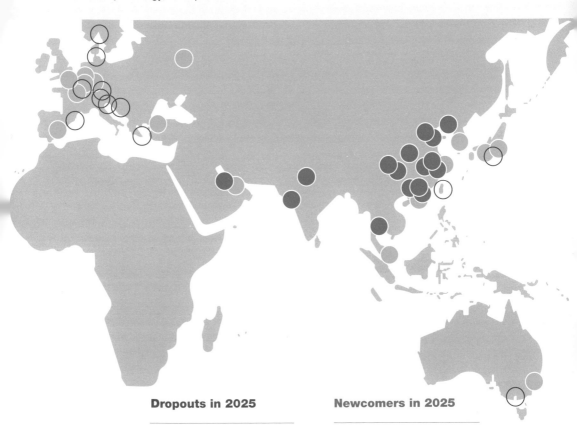

Dropouts in 2025	Newcomers in 2025
Athens	Bangkok
Barcelona	Beijing
Denver	Chengdu
Detroit	Chongqing
Hamburg	Delhi
Lille	Doha
Melbourne	Foshan
Minneapolis–St. Paul	Guangzhou
Munich	Hangzhou
Nagoya	Mumbai
Oslo	Nanjing
Rhein–Main	Shenyang
Rio de Janeiro	Shenzhen
Stuttgart	Tianjin
Taipei	Wuhan
Vienna	Xi'an

Map illustration by Celia Johnson

Applied Insight

Tools, techniques, and frameworks for managers

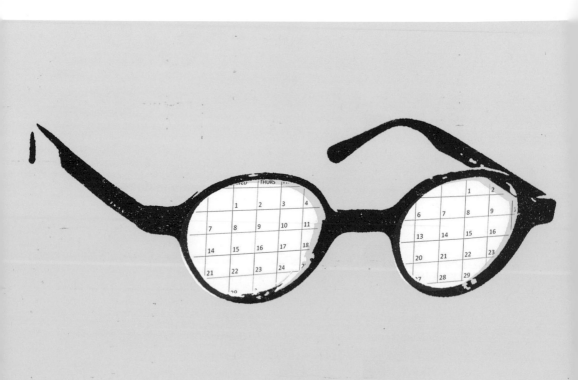

Making the most of the CEO's *last* 100 days

Christian Caspar and Michael Halbye

For the sake of their companies—and their legacies—departing chief executives should leave things in the best possible shape. Here's how.

Management literature is rich with analysis of the first 100 days of a CEO's tenure. Far less attention has been paid to a CEO's *last* 100 days. We haven't conducted systematic research on this topic, but we have seen quite a few CEO transitions over the years. And everything we've observed suggests that continuing to act as CEO until the very last day boosts the odds of leaving a company in the best shape possible and strengthening the legacy of the departing leader. Typically, in our experience, that legacy isn't fully defined until two years or so *after* the CEO steps down—and it's much more satisfying to be remembered for making tough, even unpopular, decisions that ultimately prove valuable than to leave on a high note that isn't sustained.

In most cases, incumbent CEOs know when they are likely to leave, and there is usually some time—three months to a year—between the announcement of their departure and the new CEO's start date. Many departing CEOs view this as a time to step back and avoid making major decisions or stepping on the toes of their successors. While this instinct is understandable, it reduces the likelihood of leaving the new CEO with several important advantages: a clear strategy, plenty of operating momentum, a strong management team, and a clean slate, including the firm resolution of any major outstanding operational or people challenges.

There's no simple list of actions departing CEOs should take; planning the outgoing transition is more art than science. And of course, each individual must find a transition style that's consistent with his or her personality and the organization's culture. That said, we've seen several CEOs benefit from asking themselves a few straightforward questions. The answers allow departing CEOs to create a short list of crucial actions to complete in their last days with a company.

Dan Page

Would I undertake any strategic or major organizational shifts if I had three more years ahead of me?

An incumbent CEO is likely to be knowledgeable about the strengths and weaknesses of the organization's current strategy and operations, as well as any changes that are warranted. If the incumbent doesn't act, a year or more could elapse before the new CEO is ready to do so. And in most industries today, that kind of delay can be costly. For example, a few years ago the CEO of a major high-tech firm retired without establishing clear strategic priorities for the next few years. This casual handoff, combined with the rapid pace of change in the industry and the new CEO's failure to get up to speed quickly, proved dangerous. Just two years into the new CEO's tenure, the company was lagging so far behind competitors it had to be restructured.

By contrast, the outgoing CEO of a major food and beverage company continued to push a hostile takeover—the company's largest acquisition ever—until his last day. His successor was able to complete the deal quickly and gained a strong competitive advantage thanks to the outgoing CEO's persistence. And at a logistics company, the departing CEO began a major strategic review just a few

This commentary is adapted from a recent interview with Owens conducted by McKinsey's Hans-Werner Kaas, a director in the Detroit office.

Watch the full interview on mckinseyquarterly.com.

My last 100 days

Jim Owens stepped down as the CEO of Caterpillar in June 2010 after 38 years with the global construction-equipment maker and retired as chairman four months later. He is currently a member of the President's Economic Recovery Advisory Board.

" I found out at 10 o'clock at night that I was going to be the next chairman and CEO. It was announced the next morning, and ten work days later my predecessor was moving aside. He didn't want to be a lame duck, and that's an understandable reaction.

Having spent 12 to 18 months on strategy once I got settled into the job, I felt it would be extremely beneficial to the enterprise if the

months before he left. The result was the revelation of significant weaknesses, most notably in a large business unit whose strategy was adrift. This review led that CEO directly to the next question.

Which people decisions would I make now if I had to stay for three more years?

All CEOs are concerned with the depth of talent in their organizations, particularly on the leadership team. Most are constantly trying to upgrade it, and many have a couple of replacements at the ready. Nothing is easier than not making

tough decisions near the end of one's term, falling back on the excuse that the new CEO should be free to build his or her own team. Yet such thinking can be disadvantageous to the incoming leader— who is always free to make changes and generally will benefit from starting with the strongest possible team. Sometimes the right approach means making a tough decision that will, essentially, clean the slate for the new CEO.

The outgoing CEO at the logistics company above, for example, realized he had to fire the head of the major business unit, who had been a colleague for 15 years. By doing so, he was able to take the first step toward setting that unit

person who was going to replace me knew it at least 9, 10 months ahead of time so that he could work on refreshing the strategy. So we decided we would transition when he was ready to roll out the strategy at mid-year, and he would become CEO at the end of June. He would roll out the strategy to our global supply chain so our employees, dealers, and key suppliers would get the rollout message from the chairman-elect and new CEO. By the time we got to June, I had pretty much handed over the reins.

It's not as much fun to be leaving as it is arriving. On the other hand, it's not so much about fun for the outgoing CEO as it is about a seam-

less transition and having an enterprise that has traction with the new strategy right out of the box. So, there's no time wasted, there's no big shifting of gears.

This is art more than science. A lot depends on the people and how they work the transition. As the outgoing CEO, you've got to stay engaged long enough, but you've got to know when you need to get out of the way and let the new team take over. The organization can only look at one leader at a time."

The outgoing CEO can help immensely by arranging meetings for the new leader with people who would not otherwise be on her radar screen.

on a more profitable path. We also suspect that he improved his own legacy by making this decision as soon as its necessity became clear.

....

Does the company have sufficient operational momentum to deliver strong results this year and next?

Strong performance over time requires that companies both create and respond to change: internal changes, such as new targets and initiatives, and external ones, like new market conditions and customer needs. The departing CEO should ensure that her company has a robust pipeline of activities to understand and implement change, as well as to build needed capabilities. Some activities will surely be aimed at growth, but they don't all have to be. A transportation company CEO, for example, implemented the second phase of a major cost-cutting initiative just before leaving. His successor had a far more manageable cost base when he came in.

Organizations also have a natural tendency to lose time during CEO transitions because individuals focus on topics such as what the change means for them and what the new CEO is like. One way we've

seen companies avoid slowing down is for the departing CEO, together with the management team, to document her current plans in detail, with specific accountabilities and performance milestones. That plan is then shared with the board, so the directors know where the company stands, and with her successor if one has been named. The departing CEO of a major transportation company, for example, decided not to hold a traditional last board meeting, with speeches and champagne. Instead, the CEO and his successor focused on the current status of the company and its plans and objectives for the next 12 months.

....

What do I wish I had understood better when I started in the job?

If the new CEO comes from outside the company or the industry, she will certainly have a fresh perspective; indeed, that is one major reason companies choose such a CEO. But in this situation, the departing CEO should pay particular attention to introducing her to the business. What's most crucial are tips that no one else could know. Such insights rarely emerge from typical new CEO "integration" programs, which in practice are largely ceremonial.

The outgoing CEO can help immensely by arranging meetings for the new leader with people who would not otherwise be on her radar screen but may be able to point out unexpected land mines. Think of this as an integration program with an edge: talking with several analysts who have proved themselves thoughtful critics of the company, sitting down with senior executives from a few major ex-customers who might be willing to tell the new leader things they'd previously held back about their defection, getting views from a union leader or two who will tell it like it is. Such discussions can be invaluable, and they are unlikely to happen unless the outgoing CEO mines his memory bank for a short list of high-impact discussion partners.

What's my plan for the last 100 days?

Answering questions like the ones above can help outgoing CEOs set a priority list for their last 100 days. These questions helped one recently departed CEO whittle down a list of 25 ongoing high priorities to the following 5, chosen because of their potential financial impact or because they were areas he felt he needed to clean up rather than leave as unpleasant tasks for his successor.

Explore alternative organizational models for the largest business unit.

Start concrete work on e-commerce, taking inspiration from competitors X and Y.

Secure best-practice methodology to maximize the return on the company's impending €500 million investment in support infrastructure.

Analyze the advantages and consequences of acquisition Z, which the company has long discussed but never rigorously assessed.

Accelerate efforts to reduce sourcing costs by 20 percent and implement proposed reductions in administrative and overhead costs.

● ● ●

We recognize that delivering on priorities such as these requires concentrated effort and might strike some departing CEOs as wading too far into their successors' territory. Yet in the few instances where we've seen CEOs take an active and structured approach to their last 100 days, it has been an invaluable gift to the company and to the new CEO. It also, we sense, means fewer sleepless nights for the former CEO, who will care about the company long after he has left and will rest better knowing he did all he could until the very last day. ○

Christian Caspar is a director in McKinsey's Zurich office, and **Michael Halbye** is a director in the Copenhagen office.

The power of storytelling:
What nonprofits can teach
the private sector about social media

*Learn how to harness the power of social media in this case study
excerpted from* The Dragonfly Effect. *Then hear more from the authors
in a conversation with McKinsey's Dan Singer.*

Companies are spending countless hours and millions of dollars trying to
master social media. Is this a revolutionary platform that can drive everything from customer relationships to product development—or just another
form of marketing? In a new book titled *The Dragonfly Effect*, Stanford
University marketing professor Jennifer Aaker and marketing strategist Andy
Smith seek to answer these questions by examining numerous examples
of social media at work, distilling a framework for inspiring infectious action.

One of the four "dragonfly wings" that comprise the authors' framework and
give the book its name is *engagement*, which they define as "truly making
people feel emotionally connected to helping you achieve your goals" through
storytelling, authenticity, and establishing a personal connection. Presented
here is an excerpt adapted from the book, followed by a discussion between
the authors and Dan Singer, a director in McKinsey's New York office. The
conversation focused on lessons useful for leaders seeking to boost their organizations' marketing effectiveness by engaging customers through social
media. The bottom line: using social media to capture people's attention is
different from traditional advertising, and companies that measure the
effectiveness of these new channels by simply counting Facebook fans should
rethink their approach.

Social-media engagement:
A case study from *The Dragonfly Effect*

Scott Harrison was at the top of his world. The 28-year-old New York–based nightclub and fashion promoter excelled at bringing models and hedge-fund kings together and selling them $500 bottles of vodka. He had money and power. Yet his lifestyle brought something else: emptiness. Harrison felt spiritually bankrupt.

So he walked away, volunteering to serve on a floating hospital offering free medical care in the world's poorest nations. Serving as the ship's photo-journalist, Harrison was quickly immersed in a very different world. Thousands would flock to the ship looking for solutions to debilitating problems: enormous tumors, cleft lips and palates, flesh eaten by bacteria from waterborne diseases. Harrison's camera lens brought into focus astonishing poverty and pain, and he began documenting the struggles of these people and their courage.

After eight months, he moved back to New York, but not to his former life. Aware that many of the diseases and medical problems he witnessed stemmed from inadequate access to clean drinking water, he decided to do something about it. In 2006, he founded Charity: Water, a nonprofit designed to bring clean and safe drinking water to people in developing nations.

Harrison launched the organization on his 31st birthday by asking friends to donate $31 instead of giving him a gift. It was a success—the birthday generated $15,000 and helped build Charity: Water's first few wells in Uganda. In the three years that followed, Harrison's simple birthday wish snowballed into donations that today total more than $20 million, translating into almost 3,000 water projects spanning everything from hand-dug wells and deep wells to protection for springs to rainwater harvesting. The organization has now provided clean water to more than 1.4 million people spanning 17 countries. Its success can be explained through four design principles for generating engagement with a brand through social media.

Tell a story. Harrison's personal journey—evoking themes of redemption, change, and hope—engaged others on an emotional level. By candidly discussing in media interviews and YouTube videos why and how he started Charity: Water, the thoughtful, accessible, and youthful Harrison helped viewers fall in love with him and his cause.

This case study is adapted from Jennifer Aaker and Andy Smith's *The Dragonfly Effect* (Jossey-Bass, September 2010).

Empathize with your audience. Let people engage with your brand to learn what's important to them and how it relates to your campaign. Charity: Water evoked empathy through the use of photographs and videos that revealed the urgency of the water problem in the developing world. Instead of relying just on statistics, the organization promoted compelling stories that forced people to think about what it would be like to live without access to clean water.

Emphasize authenticity. True passion is contagious, and the more authenticity you convey, the more easily others can connect with you and your cause. Because of Charity: Water's commitment to transparency, donors not only understand the history that gave rise to the organization but also know exactly where their money goes. Reports and updates on the charity's Web site connect donors directly to the results of their generosity.

Match the media with the message. How and where you say something can be as important as what you say. Charity: Water has a staff member dedicated to updating various social-media platforms and creating distinctive messages for Twitter and Facebook fan pages. The organization also relies heavily on video. One of Charity: Water's most effective video projects involved convincing Terry George, the director of the film *Hotel Rwanda*, to make a 60-second public-service announcement in which movie star Jennifer Connelly took a container to New York City's Central Park, filled it with dirty water from the lagoon, and brought it home to serve to her two children. The producers of the reality TV show *American Idol* agreed to broadcast the spot during the program, ensuring that more than 25 million viewers saw it.

Viral-video campaigns and a focus on social media help Charity: Water spread the word.

Applying the lessons beyond the social sector:
McKinsey's Dan Singer talks with the authors of *The Dragonfly Effect*

Dan Singer: *If you look at powerful social-media campaigns or initiatives, what's the essence of good storytelling?*

Jennifer Aaker: Good stories have three components: a strong beginning, a strong end, and a point of tension. Most people confuse stories with situations. They'll tell about a situation: *X* happened, *Y* happened, *Z* happened. But a good story takes *Y*, the middle part of the story, and creates tension or conflict where the reader or the audience is drawn into the story, what's going to happen next.

Treating stories as assets is an underrealized idea right now. Stories serve as glue to unify communities. Stories spread from employee to employee, from consumer to consumer, and, in some cases, from employee to consumer or consumer to employee. Stories are much more memorable than statistics or simple anecdotes and are a mechanism that allows communities to grow. Strong stories can be told and retold. They become infectious.

Jennifer Aaker is the General Atlantic Professor of Marketing at Stanford University's Graduate School of Business.

There are at least four important stories that all companies should have in their portfolio. The first is the "who am I?" story—you know, how did we get started? The second is the "vision" story, the "where are we going in the future?" This may or may not be connected to the "who are we?" story. A third is the "apology and recovery" story. In any long-term relationship, there is inevitably going to be transgression. But it is remarkable to see how few companies have thought through what a transgression is for them and how they might respond to it. The final type of story that becomes really important for corporations to have in their bank is the "personal" story: what are the personal stories that are being incubated and cultivated within the organization? This is a very different type of story. This shines a light on people rather than the organization.

Dan Singer: *Is it the story that resonates? Or is it the storyteller?*

Andy Smith: The story is the most important thing. You don't have to be famous to tell a good story. Where it really does come back to the storyteller is authenticity. People have to believe you. And you have to believe in the story yourself in order to be effective.

Andy Smith is a marketing strategist and principal at Vonavona Ventures.

Jennifer Aaker: The reason authenticity becomes important in social media is that as you think about customers or employees stepping toward a cause, it's oftentimes done when they trust the entity. When they step away from an organization, cause, or goal, it's often because they feel it's overly manufactured, overly professional, something to potentially distrust.

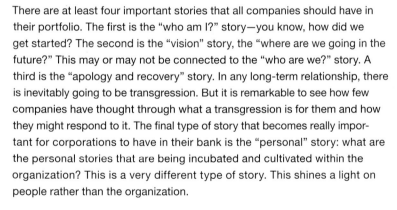

Dan Singer: *An unstated assumption is that the medium through which the communication happens is electronic—Facebook, e-mail, Twitter. As those platforms become mature and probably fairly cluttered, will people get social fatigue?*

Andy Smith: Oh, I think people have already started to show plenty of fatigue. It seems like the more things change, the shorter the life span between early adopters and people burning out. How many Twitter people can you follow?

Jennifer Aaker: There's one study that we're running right now that looks at the degree to which a subject gets asked to contribute some money or time to a cause. The number of people who delete something like this immediately from their inbox is somewhere around 95 percent. So you're already seeing people feeling inundated by "asks," especially in the social-good realm. Then there's another big group of people who feel that social media is overhyped and has gotten too much attention.

Dan Singer: *This is eerily reminiscent of traditional forms of advertising. In television, there's so much clutter that what differentiates the effective from the rest is the quality of the story and the resources of the advertiser. Would you say the same is true here? What's going to differentiate the 5 percent that get read from the 95 percent that get deleted?*

Andy Smith: For advertisers, [it will be] creativity and the depth to which they really apply the principles of understanding what's going to make people go. You literally just can't throw a switch and write a check and buy it. But you can certainly get more airplay and more attention if you nurture your community and build your followers, build your fan base, build the things that matter, and then activate them.

Jennifer Aaker: It's about the people driving the technology. You have to be cognizant of where the true power of social technology lies. It's not in the technology—it's in the people using it. ○

Listen to an extended version of the conversation between Jennifer Aaker, Andy Smith, and Dan Singer on mckinseyquarterly.com.

Kyle T. Webster

Three steps to building a better top team

Michiel Kruyt, Judy Malan, and Rachel Tuffield

When a top team fails to function, it can paralyze a whole company. Here's what CEOs need to watch out for.

Few teams function as well as they could. But the stakes get higher with senior-executive teams: dysfunctional ones can slow down, derail, or even paralyze a whole company. In our work with top teams at more than 100 leading multinational companies,[1] including surveys with 600 senior executives at 30 of them, we've identified three crucial priorities for constructing and managing effective top teams. Getting these priorities right can help drive better business outcomes in areas ranging from customer satisfaction to worker productivity and many more as well.

1. Get the right people on the team . . . and the wrong ones off

Determining the membership of a top team is the CEO's responsibility— and frequently the most powerful lever to shape a team's performance. Many CEOs regret not employing this lever early enough or thoroughly enough. Still others neglect it entirely, assuming instead that factors such as titles, pay grades, or an executive's position on the org chart are enough to warrant default membership. Little surprise, then, that more than one-third of the executives we surveyed said their top teams did not have the right people and capabilities.

The key to getting a top team's composition right is deciding what contributions the team as a whole, and its members as individuals, must make to achieve an organization's performance aspirations and then making the necessary changes in the team. This sounds straightforward, but it typically requires conscious attention and courage from the CEO; otherwise, the top team can underdeliver for an extended period of time.

That was certainly the case at a technology services company that had a struggling top team: fewer than one in five of its members thought it was highly respected or shared a common vision for the future, and only one in three thought it made a valuable contribution to corporate performance. The company's customers were very dissatisfied—they rated its cost, quality, and service delivery at only 2.3 on a 7-point scale—and the team couldn't even agree on the root causes.

A new CEO reorganized the company, creating a new strategy group and moving from a geography-based structure to one based on two customer-focused business units— for wholesale and for retail. He adapted the composition of his top team, making the difficult decision to remove two influential regional executives who had strongly resisted cross-organizational collaboration and adding the executive leading the strategy group and the two executives leading the retail and the wholesale businesses, respectively. The CEO then used a series of workshops to build trust and a spirit of collaboration among the members of his new team and to eliminate the old regional silo mentality. The team also changed its own performance metrics, adding customer service and satisfaction performance indicators to the traditional short-term sales ones.

Customers rated the company's service at 4.3 a year later and at 5.4 two years later. Meanwhile, the top team, buoyed by these results, was now confident that it was better prepared to improve the company's performance. In the words of one team member, "I wouldn't have believed we could have come this far in just one year."

....

2. Make sure the top team does just the work only it can do

Many top teams struggle to find purpose and focus. Only 38 percent of the executives we surveyed said their teams focused on work that

Determining the membership of a top team is the CEO's responsibility—and frequently the most powerful lever to shape a team's performance.

truly benefited from a top-team perspective. Only 35 percent said their top teams allocated the right amounts of time among the various topics they considered important, such as strategy and people.

What are they doing instead? Everything else. Too often, top teams fail to set or enforce priorities and instead try to cover the waterfront. In other cases, they fail to distinguish between topics they must act on collectively and those they should merely monitor. These shortcomings create jam-packed agendas that no top team can manage properly. Often, the result is energy-sapping meetings that drag on far too long and don't engage the team, leaving members wondering when they can get back to "real work." CEOs typically need to respond when such dysfunctions arise; it's unlikely that the senior team's members— who have their own business unit goals and personal career incentives— will be able to sort out a coherent set of collective top-team priorities without a concerted effort.

The CEO and the top team at a European consumer goods company rationalized their priorities by creating a long list of potential topics they could address. Then they asked which of these had a high value to the business, given where they wanted to take it, and would allow them, as a group, to add extraordinary value. While narrowing the list down to ten items, team members spent considerable time challenging each other about which topics individual team members could handle or delegate. They concluded,

for example, that projects requiring no cross-functional or cross-regional work, such as addressing lagging performance in a single region, did not require the top team's collective attention even when these projects were the responsibility of an individual team member. For delegated responsibilities, they created a transparent and consistent set of performance indicators to help them monitor progress.

This change gave the top team breathing room to do more valuable work. For the first time, it could focus enough effort on setting and dynamically adapting cross-category and cross-geography priorities and resource allocations and on deploying the top 50 leaders across regional and functional boundaries, thus building a more effective extended leadership group for the company. This, in turn, proved crucial as the team led a turnaround that took the company from a declining to a growing market share. The team's tighter focus also helped boost morale and performance at the company's lower levels, where employees now had more delegated responsibility. Employee satisfaction scores improved to 79 percent, from 54 percent, in just one year.

....

3. Address team dynamics and processes

A final area demanding unrelenting attention from CEOs is effective team dynamics, whose absence is a frequent problem: among the top teams we studied, members reported that only about 30 percent of their time was spent in "productive collaboration"—a figure that dropped even more when teams dealt with high-stakes topics where members had differing, entrenched interests. Here are three examples of how poor dynamics depress performance:

→ **The top team at a large mining company** formed two camps with opposing views on how to address an important strategic challenge. The discussions on this topic hijacked the team's agenda for an extended period, yet no decisions were made.

→ **The top team at a Latin American insurance company** was completely demoralized when it began losing money after government reforms opened up the country to new competition. The team wandered, with little sense of direction or accountability, and blamed its situation on the government's actions. As unproductive discussions prevented the top team from taking meaningful action, other employees became dissatisfied and costs got out of control.

→ **The top team at a North American financial-services firm** was not aligned effectively for a critical company-wide operational-improvement effort. As a result, different departments were taking counterproductive and sometimes contradictory actions. One group, for example, tried to increase cross-selling, while another refused to share relevant information about customers because it wanted to "own" relationships with them.

CEOs can take several steps to remedy problems with team dynamics. The first is to work with the team to develop a common, objective understanding of why its members aren't collaborating effectively. There are several tools available for the purpose, including top-team surveys, interviews with team members, and 360-degree evaluations of individual leaders. The CEO of the Latin American insurance company used these methods to discover that the members of his top team needed to address building relationships and trust with one another and with the organization even before they agreed on a new corporate strategy and on the cultural changes necessary to meet its goals (for more on building trust, see "Dispatches from the front lines of management innovation," on page 118). One of the important cultural changes for this top team was that its members needed to take ownership of the changes in the company's performance and culture and to hold one another accountable for living up to this commitment.

Correcting dysfunctional dynamics requires focused attention and interventions, preferably as soon as an ineffective pattern shows up. At the mining company, the CEO learned, during a board meeting focused on the team's dynamics, that his approach—letting the unresolved discussion go on in hopes of gaining consensus and commitment from the team—wasn't working and that his team expected him to step in. Once this became clear, the CEO brokered a decision and had the team jump-start its implementation.

Often more than a single intervention is needed. Once the CEO at the financial-services firm understood how poorly his team was aligned, for example, he held a series of top-team off-site meetings aimed specifically at generating greater agreement on strategy. One result: the team made aligning the organization part of its collective agenda, and its members committed themselves to communicating and checking in regularly with leaders at lower levels of the organization to ensure that they too were working consistently and collaboratively on the new strategy. One year later, the top team was much more unified around the aims of the operational-improvement initiative—the proportion of executives who said the team had clarity of direction doubled, to 70 percent, and the team was no longer working at cross-purposes. Meanwhile, operational improvements were gaining steam: costs came down by 20 percent over the same period, and the proportion of work completed on time rose by 8 percent, to 96.3 percent.

Finally, most teams need to change their support systems or processes to catalyze and embed change. At the insurer, for example, the CEO saw to it that each top-team member's performance indicators in areas such as cost containment and employee satisfaction were aligned and pushed the team's members to share their divisional performance data. The new approach allowed these executives to hold each other accountable for performance and made it impossible to continue avoiding tough conversations about lagging performance and cross-organizational issues. Within two years, the team's dynamics had improved, along with the company's financials—to a return on invested capital (ROIC) of 16.6 percent, from −8.8 percent, largely because the team collectively executed its roles more effectively

and ensured that the company met its cost control and growth goals.

● ● ●

Each top team is unique, and every CEO will need to address a unique combination of challenges. As the earlier examples show, developing a highly effective top team typically requires good diagnostics, followed by a series of workshops and field work to address the dynamics of the team while it attends to hard business issues. When a CEO gets serious about making sure that her top team's members are willing and able to help meet the company's strategic goals, about ensuring that the team always focuses on the right topics, and about managing dynamics, she's likely to get results. The best top teams will begin to take collective responsibility and to develop the ability to maintain and improve their own effectiveness, creating a lasting performance edge. ○

[1] For the purposes of this article, we define "top teams" as groups of executives responsible for either an entire corporation or a large business unit or division, but not boards of directors or supervisory boards.

The authors wish to acknowledge the contributions of Carolyn Aiken, a principal in McKinsey's Toronto office, and Scott Keller, a director in the Chicago office.

Michiel Kruyt is an associate principal in McKinsey's Amsterdam office, **Judy Malan** is a principal in the Johannesburg office, and **Rachel Tuffield** is an alumnus of the Sydney office.

Dispatches from the front lines of management innovation

Gary Hamel and Polly LaBarre

Meet the M-Prize winners—three case studies in management innovation honored by Gary Hamel's Management Innovation eXchange.

The Management Innovation eXchange (MIX) is a Web-based open-innovation project dedicated to catalyzing the creativity of thinkers and practitioners interested in reinventing management. That's not an undertaking for any one individual or organization—it's everybody's problem, which is why the MIX is designed as a collaborative platform both to surface bold ideas and make progress on a set of make-or-break challenges.

Earlier this year, the MIX introduced its first-ever management-innovation contest, the M-Prize, which focused on three such challenges: redefining the work of leadership, increasing trust, and taking the work out of work. MIXers from all over the world contributed hundreds of entries. Few of the submissions are world changing, some are half baked, and a couple are truly off the wall. But so many of them are bold and original, sometimes even audaciously imaginative, that they confirm our deeply held belief that everyone wins when everyone shares. Here are three of the winning stories, which offer insights for management innovators everywhere.

Judges for the M-Prize included:

Bill George, a professor at Harvard Business School and former chairman and CEO of Medtronic;

Terri Kelly, president and CEO of W. L. Gore & Associates;

John Mackey, cofounder and CEO of Whole Foods Market;

Tom Malone, a professor at MIT Sloan School of Management;

J. Leighton Read, a partner at Alloy Ventures;

Raj Sisodia, a professor of marketing at Bentley University.

McKinsey is a knowledge partner of the MIX but was not involved with the judging.

To learn more about these stories or other winning entries not described here, visit the M-Prize home page: managementexchange.com/m-prize.

Redefining leadership in public housing

Portsmouth is one of England's largest and most densely populated urban areas—once home to Charles Dickens and to Arnold Schwarzenegger and now to "17,000 blocked toilets and 100,000 dripping taps," says John Seddon, an occupational psychologist and management thinker. Several years ago, he began working closely with Owen Buckwell, who as head of housing for the Portsmouth City Council manages those toilets and taps, as well as all of the upkeep for some 50,000 people living in government-built council homes.

In late 2006, Buckwell and Seddon began pursuing a single compelling purpose: "to carry out the right repair at the right time" for tenants. The lever of change was a new management system designed to respond quickly to demand, measure value created for tenants (rather than costs or government-mandated targets), and reflect actual work flows (rather than fitting work to rigid standards and protocols). Within just a few months, Buckwell and his team built a process in which tenants could call up for service, get a real human being on the first ring, and schedule service at exactly the time they desired (not a half-day window, a two-hour window, or even a 15-minute window). The tradesperson providing the service would show up—equipped with all the correct parts required to do the job—and ask if anything else needed fixing.

Buckwell and his team accomplished this feat by shifting away from a paper-based daily printout of jobs for plumbers, glaziers, carpenters, and other craftsmen. A sophisticated visual system now matches the demands of customers (which ones want what jobs at what times) with the supply of tradespeople by highlighting when each is likely to come free from his or her current job. Large screens at headquarters provide transparency, and "the system works as a single piece flow, with each tradesman getting one job at a time" to avoid bottlenecks and delays.

The result: astonished customers, intense gratitude, hand-delivered flowers and chocolates, and a growing sense of trust between tenants and council. The story by the numbers is equally impressive: days to complete a repair dropped from 60 to 7, while the proportion of problems fixed on the first visit rose to 99 percent, from 45 percent. The proportion of calls from tenants complaining of failure shrunk to 13 percent, from 60 percent, and the tenant satisfaction rate rose dramatically to 9.93 out of 10—all while the cost per repair was slashed by more than half.

Finally, the housing council's culture has shifted from one of "learned helplessness and cheating to meet targets" to one that encourages employees to show up with their initiative and imagination fully engaged; a new ethos that emphasizes action has taken hold. "Owen always had a sneaking suspicion that people go to work to do a good job," says Seddon. "It turns out he was right."

....

Increasing trust at Microsoft

Four years ago, Ross Smith, then director of Microsoft's 85-person Windows Security Test team, conducted a series of one-on-one meetings with his people. He came away deeply impressed by the talent and enthusiasm within the team but deeply distressed that his workplace didn't come close to offering the freedom and support required for everyone to bring all of their creativity, imagination, and energy to work.

Then Smith and some colleagues stumbled upon a trove of research around the role of trust in innovative organizations. It hit them like a thunderbolt. Every quality and behavior they sought to cultivate—freedom to try new things, permission to question, the ability to see old things in a new light, support for risk taking, and a tolerance for failure—was rooted in trust. But how to create something as elusive, emotion laden, and fragile as trust?

Smith asked his group to come up with a list of behaviors that influenced trust in day-to-day work. The list reached 150 items but failed to energize the group. So Smith and his colleagues devised a simple Web-based game that walked players through a series of forced choices between trust-inducing behaviors and then compiled the collective responses to create a rank ordering of the behaviors.

With the prioritized list as a starting point, Smith encouraged the group to collaborate on a "trust playbook" wiki. The wiki included examples and scripts for specific trust-influencing behaviors, such as "praise publicly, correct privately," that had been highlighted as important. As simple as this process seemed, it opened up crucial awareness around the importance of feeding trust every day—and gave the team a vocabulary to "call out things we wouldn't normally have talked about," recalls Smith.

The playbook was just a start. Smith and his team also introduced Web-based tools for sharing information, bidding out problems, and pitching new ideas. They experimented with collaborative productivity games as a way to inject a sense of fun, improve management processes, and instill new behaviors. And they regularly reinforced the spirit of idea sharing and experimentation without fear through weekly pizza meetings, a separate forum for employees with less than two years on the job, and a book club.

What have been the results? Smith reports that the group's retention numbers saw a 20 to 50 percent rise against historic norms and peer organizations. Productivity also spiked 10 to 60 percent. Morale, as measured by "laughter in the hallways," soared. And the initiative has yielded a number of innovative offshoots. For example, an idea-sharing forum connected one team member who had built a prototype customer feedback game with another who was trying to use native language speakers to enhance the quality of international versions of Windows. The two collaborated to build a game in which people check and correct the phrasing and cultural nuances of translations. Across Microsoft, the Windows Language Quality Game attracted 4,600 players, who completed half a million tasks in just four months.

Although Smith has moved on to another part of Microsoft (as test director for Lync, a unified communications server product), his initiative continues to attract people from all around the company. From the outset, this humble, deliberately nebulous trust-building effort had a name—42Projects, in honor of Jackie Robinson's uniform number, among other things—that transcended organizational boundaries.[1] Regardless of the department or role of participants, they find in 42Projects a source of identity and collaborative energy that's rare inside large corporations.

Which trust factor is more important to you?

A simple online game helped Microsoft employees learn which trust factors mattered most.
To play the game yourself, visit defectprevention.org/trust.

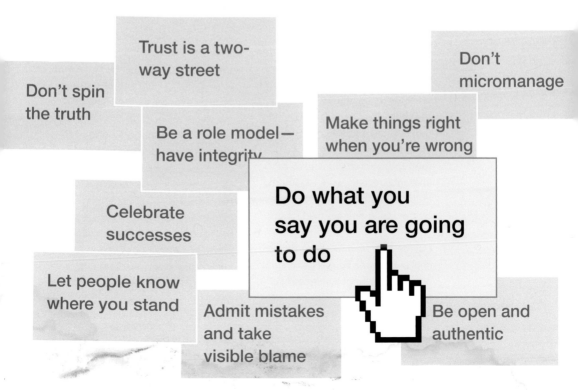

Trust is a two-way street

Don't micromanage

Don't spin the truth

Be a role model— have integrity

Make things right when you're wrong

Do what you say you are going to do

Celebrate successes

Let people know where you stand

Admit mistakes and take visible blame

Be open and authentic

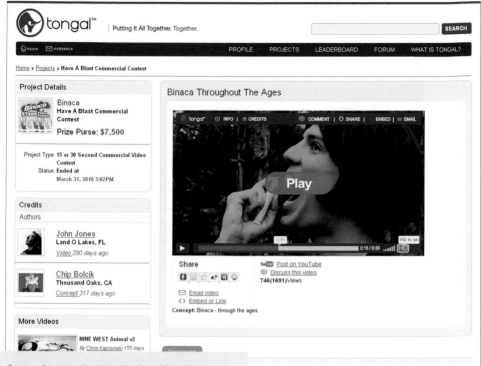

A crowdsourced, prize-winning video from Tongal highlights the benefits of alternative marketing techniques—and fresh breath.

Taking the work out of filmmaking

James DeJulio, a former Hollywood filmmaker and producer, launched Tongal in May 2009. It's a disruptive start-up aimed at revolutionizing the development of filmed content (from 30-second advertisements to feature films) by creating a platform for talented individuals to share their ideas, work together to create something that gets seen by the world, and get paid for it.

Clients offer up a deadline-driven challenge to the Tongal community— create a "future of insurance" sci-fi video for Allstate, film a favorite movie scene spoof for the makers of Binaca (a breath spray), tell an inspiring story and evangelize the cause of microlending pioneer Kiva.org. Then each project is broken down into stages. In the first (idea) phase, users submit short concepts for the project. The best five ideas advance to the next phase and the authors get a cash prize; they also earn a percentage of the prize money their submission generates in subsequent rounds.

In the second (pitch) phase, members submit more fleshed-out narratives for any of the winning ideas, and, again, the best five get a cash prize and advance. In the third phase, members create polished videos based on any of the winning pitches, and a jury of judges hand-picked for each project selects the top five for a cash award. At the same time, members can view the submissions and predict winners. The most accurate forecast gets a prize. Finally, in the exhibition phase, members compete to distribute the videos. The most viral one gets a prize—and creator, client, and community "marketer" all win.

In the first year of operation, Tongal has attracted 5,000 registered members from 40 countries around the world and so far has run 24 contests, with prize purses as large as $15,000. Clients like both the product (not nearly as polished as that of agencies, but full of unexpected ideas and edge) and the economics ($5,000 for five videos and their distribution on the Web versus $630,000 for airing a 30-second prime-time spot).

Tongal isn't just a disruptive business model; it's also an instructive design for work in an age when architecting participation is every leader's job. Tongal distinguishes itself from most crowd-sourcing platforms by the fact that you can't win without building on the ideas and contributions that came before (or after) you. Tongal's designers strive to create connection and transparency wherever possible on the site, from its leaderboard to vibrant forums for each project. What's more, you don't have to win to win. Whether you submit an idea in the first round, create a video, or just jump in to promote a winner in the exhibition phase, you still reap rewards, connect with the creative community, and stretch some creative muscles.

As inspiring and instructive as stories like these are, they are just a start. At the MIX, we dream of organizations that can spontaneously renew themselves—where the drama of change is not accompanied by the wrenching drama of a turnaround, where innovation pulses through every activity, where every individual feels inspired by noble goals, and where collaborative cultures breed intense involvement. But of course, these aren't just dreams: they are do-or-die challenges for every organization that hopes to thrive in the future. o

[1] Jackie Robinson was the first African American Major League Baseball player. He played second base for the Brooklyn Dodgers from 1947 to 1956 and was elected to the Baseball Hall of Fame in 1962.

Gary Hamel is Visiting Professor of Strategic and International Management at the London Business School and the innovation architect at the Management Innovation Exchange (MIX). **Polly LaBarre** is a coauthor of *Mavericks at Work* and the editorial director of the MIX.

Extra Point

The insight deficit

A fresh strategic insight—something your company sees that no one else does—is one of the foundations of competitive advantage. It helps companies focus their resources on moves that separate them from the pack. That makes the results below, based on a recent survey of 2,135 global executives, interesting: only about a third believed their strategies rested on unique and powerful insights. That figure was dramatically lower than the average—62 percent—for nine other tests we asked executives to measure their strategies against.

Your strategy rests on novel data and insights not available to competitors, % of respondents[1]

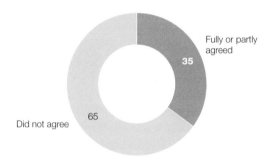

Fully or partly
agreed

35

65

Did not agree

[1] Respondents who answered "don't know" are excluded.

What's more, only 14 percent of surveyed executives placed novel insights among the top three strategic influencers of financial performance. One likely explanation: the widespread availability of information and adoption of sophisticated strategy frameworks creates an impression that "everyone knows what we know and is probably analyzing the data in the same ways that we are." The danger is obvious: if strategists question their ability to generate novel insights, they are less likely to reach for the relative advantages that are most likely to differentiate them from competitors. ○

For more on the role of insight in strategy, see Chris Bradley, Martin Hirt, and Sven Smit's article, "Have you tested your strategy lately?" on page 40; as well as Richard Rumelt's article, "The perils of bad strategy," on page 30. For the complete survey results, see "Putting strategies to the test: McKinsey Global Survey results," on mckinseyquarterly.com.